Theory Building for Learning How to Learn

D1073687

Studies in Educational Policy

THEORY BUILDING
FOR LEARNING HOW TO LEARN

EDITED BY
ROBERT M. SMITH

EDUCATIONAL STUDIES PRESS
CHICAGO, ILLINOIS

DEPARTMENT OF LEADERSHIP AND EDUCATIONAL POLICY STUDIES
NORTHERN ILLINOIS UNIVERSITY
DEKALB, ILLINOIS

The Department of Leadership and Educational Policy Studies, Northern Illinois University, in cooperation with Educational Studies Press, a constituent unit of the Center for the Advanced Study of Education, Chicago 60611

Published 1988
Printed in the United States of America
5 4 3 2 1

Cover design by Mark J. Rattin

Distributed by the LEPS Department, 325 Graham Hall, Northern Illinois University, DeKalb, Illinois, 60115

Library of Congress Cataloging-in-Publication Data

Smith, Robert McCaughan, 1925-

   Theory building for learning-how-to-learn /Robert M. Smith, editor.
   p. 152 cm.
   Bibliography; p.
   Includes index.
   1. Learning—Congresses. 2. Learning, Psychology of—Congresses.
3. Continuing education—Congresses. I. Title.

ISBN 0-934328-07-2 (lib.ed.)
ISBN 0-934328-08-0 (pbk.)

LB1060.S65 1987   370'.15 23   87-27618

Contents

PREFACE

This report attempts to capture the substantive essentials and the climate of a meeting in 1986 of fourteen persons from six nations to explore the nature and implications of the learning-how-to-learn concept and process (see roster, p. ix). The conferees had previously undertaken relevant research and writing on the subject and agreed that a theory-building or state-of-the-art meeting was long overdue. Funding for the conference came from Northern Illinois University and Cambridge Press.

The stated purposes of the conference were to explore these questions:

1. What is known about Learning-How-to-Learn?
2. What are significant knowledge gaps?
3. What information dissemination would be desirable if resources permitted?
4. What educational policy changes can be recommended?
5. What post-conference activity might be appropriate?

A collection of materials on various aspects of the subject was sent to the principals for pre-conference perusal along with a statement of purposes and tentative topics. A description of format and rationale for its nature was also provided. No papers or formal presentations were involved, and one person candidly confessed to "a little trepidation at not having the safe option of reading from a prepared paper." The heart of the format was conversations which extended over some five days. Participant-observers were present at three of these sessions. Two public symposia in the evening treated single topics: "European Contributions to Learning-How-to-Learn"; and "The Role of the School in Learning-How-to-Learn."

Because of the informal, conversational nature of most of the conference, it was not possible to produce a verbatim transcript. At times, important results from the untaped conversations of two and three person subgroups were only available from notes or reports when all fourteen principals re-assembled. This report, therefore, represents data of three kinds: (1) short lectures to a large audience; (2) slightly edited sections of lengthy periods of conversation by the principals; and (3) bits and pieces culled from here and there to capture something or a topic touched on in passing. All of these factors also help explain the uneven quantity of person-specific information found in this report.

The results of the conference exceeded expectations. The feasibility of conceptualizing learning-how-to-learn as a universal, lifelong matter was confirmed. A heuristic model was developed that describes and links a wide variety of elements previously known or believed to be related to more effective lifelong learning—a paradigm that distinguishes the different intentions and contexts of learning-how-to-learn. Relevant competencies were identified and linked to knowledge and institutional domains. And desirable applications of the concept and process were explored with regard to home, school, college, community, and workplace.

In addition to the principals themselves, who received no honoraria for the conference, many persons have made outstanding contributions to the conference and to the genesis of this report. They include Gregory Bowes, Dennis Gooler, Steve Johnson, John LaTourette, William Moore, Roslyn Randall, Edwin Simpson, Glenn Smith, Patricia Wolf Smith, Howard Swan, Judy Taylor, William

Young, and Jerold Zar. The contributions of Alan Knox, Glenn Smith, Pat Smith, and Dana Maxfield were critical.

Robert M. Smith

IDEAS WELL-EXPRESSED

How long will it take for us to conclude that learning-how-to-learn is the only education worth pursuing for students, for educators, and for society?

Patricia Cross

In the past, learning-how-to-learn has too often been limited to helping people survive in the educational system—a little like trying to help people learn to breathe during a nuclear winter.

Alan Knox

We're not creating a separate kind of learning; what we're really talking about is more active and more conscious learning in every context by everyone in society—for me that's a wonderful gift.

Mark Cheren

Somehow we have to communicate to people that learning is just the most exciting way to be in the world and that learning-how-to-learn is an incredibly important topic.

Maurice Gibbons

What learning-how-to-learn gives you is a kind of learning capital that you accumulate in the process of learning and can bank—providing that the learning experience is sufficiently rich.

Dai Hounsell

As I see it, learning-how-to-learn is a lifelong process; I don't think one reaches at any point the current state-of-the-art of learning-how-to-learn.

Malcolm Knowles

CONFERENCE ROSTER
PRINCIPALS

Philip Candy
University of New England, Australia

Ronald Cervero
University of Georgia

Mark Cheren
Sangamon State University

K. Patricia Cross
Harvard University

Ravindra H. Dave
UNESCO Institute for Education, Hamburg

Maurice Gibbons
Simon Fraser University

Virginia Griffin
Ontario Institute for Studies in Education

Dai Hounsell
University of Edinburgh

Malcolm Knowles
North Carolina State University

Alan Knox
University of Wisconsin-Madison

Dana Maxfield (Assistant Chair)
Northern Illinois University

Jean Moon
University of Wisconsin-Milwaukee

Roger Säljö
Linkoping University, Sweden

Robert M. Smith (Conference Chair)
Northern Illinois University

OBSERVER-PARTICIPANTS

David Alexander
The Northern Institute, Anchorage, Alaska

Gregory Bowes
University of New Mexico

Jane Evanson
Alaska Pacific University

Sharan Merriam
University of Georgia

Wesley Schmidt
Northern Illinois University

Merlyn Behr
Northern Illinois University

OPENING REMARKS
BY
THE CHAIR

The encouragement and support of all thirteen of you have meant a very great deal. I am almost certain this will be a successful conference, although I'm not yet sure that it will be an important conference.....you don't know that at this point.

The importance will probably be a function of leadership and participation—especially of the rate at which we can establish communication, a bit of trust, and some decision-making and concensus reaching skills, all of which groups normally take a long time to develop. I'm sure we'll have them by the end of our deliberations, but it would really help if we could achieve them very early on. Of course, we have some highly skilled "process people" here—the room is full of them, and I am sure we will succeed in that area.

Learning-how-to-learn is really in the air right now, no matter what label you put on it. Here are some examples:

> 1. I was recently at a kind of research and development center in Santa Fe, New Mexico, operated by Wilson Learning Corporation with a direct link-up to some educational psychology people at the University of Minnesota. They were telling me that their goal is to increase adult learning power ten-fold in ten years through applications of interactive media. I happened to meet there the corporate training director for Burger King (which I assume devotes considerable resources to education), and he said, "You know we think where it's at right now

is learning-how-to-learn."

2. In a project in Alberta that I've been involved in, many of the adult basic education people there are shifting, taking a real interest not only in imparting basic skills but in really enhancing the learning abilities and capabilities of these students as they go through the programs. They are doing it in a very systematic and exciting way, translating it into curriculum.

3. I recently talked with the director of popular education for Nicaragua—an interesting man who has "only a bachelor's degree"—and has one of the biggest jobs as far as education goes in Latin America. (You may recall that in Nicaragua, learning-how-to-learn was listed as one of the five key national educational goals when the republic was established—one of the rallying slogans.) This gentleman, Eduardo Baez, said that learning-how-to-learn is more important than learning subject matter. Well, I asked him what he meant by it, and he said, "Problem posing, problem solving, critical thinking, becoming aware of contradictions and processes, understanding concepts and principles, understanding that knowledge can be played with and created by non-experts, understanding that the learner is the most important resource in the teaching-learning transaction, understanding the need to act after one gains new information."

4. In a recent interview in *Psychology Today,* an expert in bio-chemistry said, "I'm learning to learn about the bio-chemistry of memory." All of these contribute to the "our house has many mansions" notion. Maybe you wish I'd stop building the rooms on the mansion so we could start focusing; I promise to stop soon.

5. In *The Aquarian Conspiracy,* Marilyn Ferguson calls for a new paradigm of learning that has as its first assumption emphasis on learning-how-to-learn.

6. At a recent ASTD (American Society for Training and Development) conference there was a section called "Learning-How-to-Learn to Sell." That's taking it quite a way.

The basic concept goes back a long time of course. In *Learning How to Learn: Applied Theory for Adults,* I mentioned that Benjamin Franklin figured it out—trained the collaborative group that he set up because he knew they weren't going to get far unless they paid some attention to process. The distinguished psychologist Alfred Binet wrote in 1909, "What children should learn first is not subjects ordinarily taught, however important; they should be given lessons in will, attention, discipline, before they get exercises in grammar. They need to be exercised in mental orthopedics (maybe that's the rubric we should use); they must learn how to learn." One of the early leaders in my discipline, adult education, Joseph Hart, in *Light from the North: the Danish Folk High Schools,* said: "We have plenty of men and women who can teach what they know; we have very few who can teach their own capacity to learn."

A final thought concerns the distinction between education and learning. I suppose they've always been used with great, what shall I say, flexibility; but lately the lack of precision is troubling to me. We really have enough semantic confusion I would think, without people talking about (for example) free learning, good learning, mature learning, "my own learning," reasons for learning, methods of learning, state policies for learning, and unlearning one's previous learning. I personally don't like "higher learning"—it suggests institutions in the Himalayas or Rockies.

And we talk about a learning experience and voluntary learners. Then we encounter somebody saying "Well you know, education begins at birth." I thought learning began at birth; maybe education does too. Maybe these distinctions aren't important. Maybe they are—for our purposes here at any rate.

PURPOSES AND AGENDA

The conference exhibited at least two agendas: one generated prior to the meeting and another that emerged from the early conversations. The first was developed largely by the chairpersons from reviewing the relevant literature and obtaining suggestions from the principals. The second arose from the expressed concerns of the principals when they sat down to explore a complex and multi-faceted concept that has emerged from research, theory building, and practice.

PRE-CONFERENCE STATEMENTS

The overall conference purposes were stated in advance in the form of five broad questions:

1. What is known about Learning-How-to-Learn?
2. What are significant knowledge gaps?
3. What information dissemination would be desirable if resources permitted?
4. What educational policy changes can be recommended?
5. What post-conference activity might be appropriate?

Attached were these relevant issues expressed as questions for exploration:

1. Is Learning-How-to-Learn the best umbrella term to employ?
2. How is Learning-How-to-Learn best defined?
3. Is a generic theory of Learning-How-to-Learn needed? Feasible?
4. Which established learning, change, and development theories have heuristic implica-

tions for Learning-How-to-Learn research and practice?

5. What is the role of motivation in Learning-How-to-Learn?

6. In what ways are Learning-How-to-Learn in pre-adulthood and adulthood related?

7. How are self-directedness, self-directed learning, and self-directed education best conceptualized for Learning-How-to-Learn research and training purposes?

8. If Learning-How-to-Learn were to become a top priority of preschool, elementary, secondary, and higher educators, what institutional changes might be appropriate?

9. To what extent is it appropriate to regard Learning-How-to-Learn as empowerment?

10. In what respects do Learning-How-to-Learn theory and practice appear to be culture bound?

11. What are core competencies for lifelong learning?

This additional list of topics (some of which overlap or might be subsumed under questions previously listed) was also distributed before the conference:

1. The role of educational agencies in fostering learning skill and a positive orientation to lifelong learning

2. How the learner's conception of what knowledge and learning "are" affect personal learning and study strategies

3. Encouraging self-directedness in those who participate in the educational programs of schools, colleges, and other organizations

4. Imparting subject matter knowledge while enhancing students' learning skills at the same time

5. Training theory and designs for fostering group inquiry, problem-solving, and teamwork
6. Learning style diagnosis as a tool for better understanding of self as learner
7. Learning-How-to-Learn applications of state-of-consciousness psychology, the repertory grid, learning conservations, and reciprocal teaching
8. Applications of Learning-How-to-Learn theory and practice in training and human resource development programs
9. The cross-cultural aspects of Learning-How-to-Learn
10. Training for reflective and critical thinking
11. Fostering metacognitive skills in the early years and adulthood
12. Helping people to learn more systematically from everyday experience
13. Learning-How-to-Learn implications and uses of interactive electronic technologies.

In retrospect this appears an all but overwhelming menu for such a short repast. However, the assumption was that the principals would, in the last analysis, deal with those matters that held interest for them as individuals, sub-groups, and a total group once those interests became expressed and modified through formal and informal interaction.

EMERGING INTERESTS AND CONCERNS

When they first assembled, some of the principals identified "particular foci and emphases regarding learning-how-to-learn" that they wished to pursue at the conference and described some relevant personal experience and background.

MALCOLM KNOWLES: I'm coming in with two primary interests. One is pooling our knowledge about the skills involved in self-directed learning, in learning-how-to-learn; what do we need to learn in order to be better learners. And what more do we need to know? Where are our gaps? And then how to create learning experiences for developing those skills. That's one big category. The other is the implications of this for the reorganization or restructuring of schooling in grades K (Kindergarten) through sixteen, especially grades twelve or thirteen through sixteen. So it's needed skills for learning, how to develop them, and what more do we need to know about needed skills.

I first got hooked on the reorganization of schools in 1972 when we had our first task force at the UNESCO Institute for Education on lifelong learning. Then a couple of years ago I was a part of another task force with Ravi Dave being—not just the moderator—but the guru.

PATRICIA CROSS: How people learn to make maximum use of the way in which they're taught is one of my big interests. For example, how can a person being presented information entirely through videotape adapt to the situation and get the most from it? How can people be helped to make the most of any educational or learning situation they encounter?

VIRGINIA GRIFFIN: I am very interested in the skills for learning-how-to-learn. I'm also interested in looking at whether or not the levels of learning make a difference in what the required skills are—if there's a difference, for example, between instrumental learning and emancipatory learning and the appropriate skills involved.

I'm also interested in "alternate" ways to learn, and I'm curious about how to integrate them with self-directed learning. Since many people don't know some of these ways to learn, they need to be helped to learn how to learn through such means as imagery, dreams, and fantasy.

RAVINDRA DAVE: I am interested in many of the aspects mentioned already, and I also think that learning-how-to-learn takes us beyond the aspects already mentioned. We should begin to see not only the implications for education (or learning, or schooling) but also some implications and related factors that lie outside of education. It depends of course on how do you define education. We should consider some extra-educational factors that are related to society, societal developments, technology, and human resource development. We might wish to try to build a bridge between extra-educational factors and the forces that prompt us to consider concepts like self-direction, learning-how-to-learn and so on. Thus we might need to build a broader base before going into it.

My second point is very much connected to the first one and is related to the question of life and living. I strongly believe that it is necessary to bring in the essential problem of life itself—the quality of life for instance, or, to be more precise, what happens as a result of a variety of developments in the name of organization. And, as a result of all this development and the type of education and learning that we encourage, what is really the impact on the quality of life? How is learning-how-to-learn connected with quality of life? We should wrestle with this because it is a fundamental issue. So I would like to see that we go into some extra-educational events, do not ignore the issues of life, and then try to relate learning with life in a variety of ways in present and future contexts.

I might add that UNESCO has been very much interested in the notion of what it described early on as lifelong education. And, at the UNESCO Institute for Education where I work, we took up the challenge of trying to understand the concept of lifelong education. We have sought to identify some of the characteristics of the concept, develop some basic ideas in the name of foundations of lifelong education, and then work out implications for the school curriculum and for the non-formal and informal systems of learning. We have tried to understand how learning occurs in this broader framework—in the home, in the school, at the work place, in the community, and through various other situations and structures, such as the media, national events, social events, religious events and so on. On the basis of this, there are some implications for teacher education for instance—to raise such basic questions as who is a teacher and who is a learner? Are the relationships between the teacher and the learner of the same hierarchical quality that evolved over hundreds of years, or are the relationships changing? What of the new roles and responsibilities of the teacher? What are the parental roles and so forth and so on? So this is an area in which UNESCO is very much interested.

There are a number of programs and projects that have been carried out in the first decade. Now we are moving more towards the developing countries where the problems are somewhat different from the problems that we have here, let us say, in the United States. There we find that some 800 million adults above the age of 15 are illiterate. What is the significance there of life-long learning, learning-how-to-learn, self-direction and so on? What is the meaning of them in this situation.

We are also going into the concept of what we call horizontal learning, where we try to relate school learning, learning in the community, and learning in the home—to see how learning can be viewed not merely as school-based or home-based but how interactive relationships are and can be established.

These are just a few examples of interests of UNESCO and the UNESCO Institute for Education.

We have now accordingly brought out about twenty-five publications on lifelong education; recently we brought out fifteen publications on post-literacy and continuing education, which is again in the framework of lifelong education for developing countries. So there is now considerable literature about what we've found out. The Council of Europe has also been very much interested in these questions (and in fact did work on them before UNESCO did) and also developed some publications. We work closely with the OECD and collaborate in training teachers.

MARK CHEREN: Expanding on the concept of a larger context—beyond the schools—I have been working in human resource development for most of the last eight years. I'm interested in the topic that is raised in some of the reading material sent to us concerning what terms and frameworks are really most helpful for people to relate to learning-how-to-learn. I have been experimenting with the use of "situational learning" (instead of "self-directed learning") as a broad framework within which people could comfortably relate to what we're talking about. Within a larger context of self-managed development, I talk about situational learning so that people can buy in—in much the same way that "situational" management has replaced "participatory" management as the religion of management theory.

To me, situational learning implies that anybody can take the initiative, anybody can have control and percentages of control can be shared in various contexts, to various extents—for example between an individual and a resource person, or between groups of learners and one or more resource people. The point is that the issue of control implies self-directed learning. We have gotten people into these all or nothing games of adult learner, child learner—

you have control or you have total responsibility, I don't have any role as a teacher, and so on. Those kinds of confusions. I'm interested in what we can do to find terms that make it easier for people to understand what we really mean, and enter in comfortably without feeling like they're playing our game with our labels. I think that's particularly important in learning in the world as opposed to learning in schools. I'm looking forward to our talking about that together. I'm also interested in whether or not there is a better overall term for learning-how-to-learn itself. I'm expecting this to be an exciting place to look at what terms truly might empower people in the way we have talked in the past about wanting to empower people.

I'm also interested in preparing people for learning in the world of work—learning through, for example, the yearly performance appraisal cycle, through development planning as it relates to how one interacts with one's supervisor and with peers in the work situation. It seems to me there might be value in talking to local school boards and with legislators about preparing people for learning in the workplace as opposed to talking only in our neat educational constructs, which they have often thought of as overly abstract. We may find that we can bring about virtually the same kinds of substance, but in the language that then prepares people to function more practically. Right now many are not functioning well, from what I can see, in the world of work. Instead of being afraid to be corrupted by the world of work, we might consider how applications there can give us real leverage in other areas.

PHILIP CANDY: I'd like to state two things. One of them is my belief that learning-how-to-learn or whatever we call that phenomenon, is not the same as self-directed or auto-didactic learning (or whatever you call that phenomenon). I feel uncomfortable using those two sets of terms interchangeably. The second thing is to test a hunch that learning to learn is a process and not a product and that it's contextually grounded. It seems that some people have written and thought about learning to learn as a package of transmittable skills without reference to the context within which a learning model might be interpreted. One could start with conceptual analysis of the relationship between autonomy, self-directed learning, and auto-didactic learning. There are four actors in this play; one of them is called adult education; one of them is called autonomy; one of them is called auto-didactic learning; and one of them is called learner control.

RONALD CERVERO: The concept of learning-how-to-learn is awfully mushy in my mind. If we come out of here with a definition that at least half of us can agree on I'll be impressed, particularly as it relates to self-directed learning. So I guess I feel a need to get some clear clarification on that.

Two other issues interest me. One goes beyond learning-how-to-learn. It's something that I have been doing a fair amount of research and reading in right now: the relationship between the individual and society and how education mediates that role. Of course there are at least two points of view: (1) that education is an empowering kind of process that gives people more skill, advantages, and social status; (2) that education is a means of maintaining a system of inequality in society.

If we change schools to a learning-how-to-learn system, how would that change the relationship between the individual and society and the role that adult education plays in it? Is the concept of self-directed learning and/or learning-how-to-learn a way out of this dilemma?

Over the last six or seven years I have been researching the area of continuing education for professional groups, and of course this learning to learn concept is discussed quite a bit among professionals—as a result of the rapid obsolescence of knowledge and other factors. A student of mine has proposed what I guess may be a new way of looking at the concept of self-directed learning. We often talk about self-directed learning as a set of processes or skills. Our thought was that this notion might be a bit limiting and that we might better see self-directed learning as a personality construct—that it is not limited to a specific set of skills or to self-instruction and is not merely program planning applied to the individual. Rather it may be something internal to the person that causes an individual to engage in activities that broaden the perception of life. So I'd like to explore learning-how-to-learn as a set of skills and also as a personality matter, something more fundamental.

MAURICE GIBBONS: One breathes in and one breathes out. When I breathe in I am concerned about really finding out something very specific that I can get my hands on. I'm interested in applications to schooling, personal development, and the spiritual side of the whole thing. When I breathe out I'm concerned about how expansive this role [learning-how-to-learn] really is. So on the one hand I'd like to be much more concrete, much more focused; I'm hoping to get a lot of new ideas (it's already started - through a wonderfully rich morning and afternoon prior to the conference's convening). On the other hand, as one breathes out, one sees that much of what we are talking about really is life; there is no aspect of life that isn't touched by self-direction and by learning.

So on the one hand we want to enclose it, while on the other hand we need to expand it to include not only our own immediate experience, not only our school experience, not only our experience in business, but internationally, globally—the whole concern about how people everywhere have the rights and need opportunities to learn and the roles they play.

I guess it really is important to me to start to put some structure on our topic. What is the best one can imagine coming out of this meeting in a realistic way? I'd be quite willing to be cooperative with the decision we might make about what is a really vital question in this area. But if we could start to examine it together, could we really make a difference? I'd be willing to bend my personal interest in that direction if we feel it can. What is the key question here, what's the thing that if we could crack, would open it in the most wonderful way for all of us so that on Wednesday when we leave we say, "Damn, that was pretty good! We really did something; I'm different; I have a new concept, a new framework to work with, and a wonderful network of people to continue to examine that framework with."

I'm also very interested, right now, in the practical side of delivering services to people who really are in desperate need of empowerment—both locally and globally. I keep coming back to these global issues of the decaying environment, of suppressed people, of potential conflict, of a future that is hurtling at us at an incessant rate and destroying all kinds of institutions and upsetting people to the point of what looks like societal decay.

JEAN MOON: I think what Maurice suggests is that to get at the implications of learning-how-to-learn you almost have to work together. You want to be practical and yet there are so many other aspects that have to be tended to. Personally I have an interest in schools. My specific interest is not only restructuring the schools but to develop processes to go along with learning-how-to-learn—looking at teaching as a profession and how it relates to that concept. Right now I'm in the midst of dissertation research which focuses on teachers' self-perception of their learning, their learning styles, and the interrelationships.

As some of you have mentioned, I'm not totally convinced that learning-how-to-learn can be compres-
sed into a set of skills. I think there's a huge developmental component here; I don't know exactly what
it is, but I think it has an impact. I also think that the
contextual questions are important when it comes
to learning-how-to-learn. My research on teachers
and learning in the classroom offers evidence of
that. I'm also interested in the tacit dimensions of
learning-how-to-learn—whether it's a personality
construct; I don't know exactly what it is, but there's
something relevant in the inner processes of
learning.

ROGER SALJO: My interest is primarily philosophical. I
am interested in the concept of learning itself—what
counts as learning in a society, and what are the
specific traditions and technological prerequisites
for defining and identifying certain processes of
learning—in particular the distinction between formalized learning (the kind that takes place in
schools) and other kinds that may or may not be
recognized as acts of learning.

I've been doing research in how people act or behave (depending on what theory you subscribe to)
in formal educational situations where they rely on
a sort of literate mode of construing knowledge. I'm
very much involved in the question of what kind of
competencies occur or need to develop out of such
formal interactions as opposed to other kinds of interaction that people don't identify.

So I think that for me this interest in learning is very
much a question of unlearning what we're supposed
to know about. The point of some of the research I
have been involved in with Dai Hounsell has been
simply to describe and give an accurate account
of what people in fact *do* without describing it as
learning—trying to get at what they do, what their
aims or goals are, how they tackle the problems.
Competencies can be many different things—for

example, learning to handle formal tasks in a very simple way. This would be quite different from the professional qualities or competencies which have to do with making judgements, dealing with complex situations, handling people, and the kinds of important skills which are not necessarily the direct product of formal training.

DAI HOUNSELL: Well, it seems to me that one matter would be absolutely fundamental, and that is the whole issue of transfer. I occasionally find myself at conferences (usually not in the formal sessions but in informal conversation) when somebody makes a comment which implies or assumes transferrability. One learns a skill in a certain context and it is applicable somewhere else. And it seems to me that the whole question of transfer is a total unknown, that we make very many assumptions about what is transferrable from one context to another. The broader danger it seems to me with learning-how-to-learn is its becoming a sort of holy grail of life itself—if you find this mysterious essence and you take it on forward then you have the ultimate transfer credit card, cashable everywhere, if you like. I think we should be thinking in terms of very clear limits on what we can take from one situation and use somewhere else.

I'm also (like Roger Säljö) interested in the distinction between learning and studying. We can look at most educational situations and define learning as, shall we say, something like a quest for meaning and define studying as something like what is necessary in order to survive and do what the institution requires. We find very often that those two are in conflict with one another. So if we actually train or help students to learn how to learn this may be dysfunctional in terms of their educational achievement. So, if we are intervening, somehow or other we've got to teach students how to study as well as how to learn, if they're to both grow and survive.

It also seems to me that it's possible, then, to make some rough and ready counterpart between that distinction between learning and studying and teaching and instructing. And I would like to preserve the term teaching for creating the conditions under which people can search for meaning.

One of my major interests then is working with students, both individually and in groups to help them learn how to learn. The other is doing research into learning, mostly at the undergraduate level. I always find it very, very hard to actually relate those two things because in a sense learning that goes on in an educational setting is incredibly complex and difficult to understand. It seems to me that some of the things that are demanded of people as learners, even though they seem narrowly academic, actually involve a quite fundamental reappraisal of self. As concerns the matter of competencies, even in the setting of educational institutions, I believe that we're not talking about some generic set of skills to be used in all situations, but rather a set of competencies which take different forms in different disciplines and educational contexts.

CONSENSUS ABOUT TASKS

These remarks by the principals have shown that many of the agenda questions developed prior to the conference were of interest to them as they began their conversations. In addition, we have seen expressed considerable interest in (1) the relationship between learning and learning-how-to-learn; (2) distinguishing self-directed learning from learning-how-to-learn; (3) defining learning-how-to-learn; (4) the role of personality and human development; (5) generic competencies versus content and context-specific proficiencies; (6) the concept's relevance to societal, social, and philosophical issues.

Summarizing the interests, concerns, and possible items thus expressed in the principals' first dialogue session, one person (Gibbons) said:

> Implicit in the great diversity of what we said is that we don't have a clear idea of what the domain of this field is; [that is]. . . the domain of knowledge that we are here to talk about, if indeed that's an appropriate title for it. What are the boundaries and what does it contain?

Soon after this the conferees agreed that they would undertake to:

1. Define the domain of learning-how-to-learn
2. Develop a paradigm of the learning-how-to-learn process
3. Compile some principles, rules, or laws governing that process

The next section presents much of the discussion related to the first task. The paradigm that emerged is described in section IV. Time ran out before the third task could be systematically addressed, and it was flagged as a major research need.

EXPLORING THE DOMAIN OF LEARNING-HOW-TO-LEARN

The question posed here was as follows: Recognizing that many or all of the agenda items identified may be important, if you were to suggest what is at the essence of the domain, what is most important to hold on to and clearly understand about learning-how-to-learn, what would it be? What would you nominate?

Some Essences

THE CONTENT/PROCESS DISTINCTION

ROBERT SMITH: It is important for both the educator and the learner to be able to understand and pay attention to the distinction between content [subject matter] and [learning associated] process.

RAVINDRA DAVE: My concern is with the word distinction. I think it's not just a distinction but [the understanding of] an interactive relationship between content and process.

UNDERSTANDINGS ABOUT MODES AND METHODS

RAVINDRA DAVE: Through group work, through individual work, through straight presentation and the like, the learner begins to realize that there are different modes of learning. And as time passes he internalizes the fact that learning can occur in different ways, by using different modalities, using different styles. Now that process of internalization, of understanding different styles of learning and relating these different styles to different kinds of learning— that internalization or understanding is essential to learning-how-to-learn.

UNDERSTANDINGS ABOUT KNOWLEDGE AND MEANING

PHILIP CANDY: If we're looking for irreducible atoms, one thing I would like to advocate is [the importance of understanding] that meaning is personally constructed, and that knowledge is socially constructed.

DAI HOUNSELL: Learning-how-to-learn is both contextually and content bound in very very important ways. One's price for the higher education experience, for example in a British type context, is to concentrate on individualistic activities, and neglect—something that has been missing right along in that culture—the ability to work collaboratively. It doesn't seem to me then that you will have acquired the skills to operate in a situation which demands collaboration. In the same way it seems to me that content is noticeably a very important influence, and I'd like to suggest that in a sense the learning-how-to-learn demands of, say, physics are not the same as those of local history, or wind surfing, or Sumo wrestling.

CHANGES IN COGNITIVE STRUCTURES

ALAN KNOX: Is there anybody who has meant by the phrase learning-how-to-learn, learning how to make your mind work in such a way that it processes information and results in learning in the sort of psychologists' black box sense? It seems to me that if anybody does, we ought to explore it further; otherwise learning-how-to-learn is a misnomer, and it's [only] learning how to study if it doesn't include learning how to acquire and process information.

RON CERVERO: There's a whole literature on meta-cognition that talks about people's strategies for understanding how they view the world and how they change those conceptions of the world. That's not what we're talking about here, are we?

MALCOLM KNOWLES: I'm including that.

PHILIP CANDY: For me, learning to learn is an interpretive process aimed at increasing people's ability to interpret reality and that makes it a meta-cognitive process—a complex higher-order process.

A LIFELONG MATTER

DAI HOUNSELL: You never stop learning-how-to-learn.

RAVINDRA DAVE: As the individual grows from childhood to adolescence and then to youth and then to adulthood, how can he or she master the techniques and processes of acquiring knowledge, of building attitudes, rebuilding them, developing a variety of skills that ultimately lead to becoming a real master of one's own learning? How can this be done? How can this be learnt? That seems to me to be the real challenge facing this group.

ACQUIRING CERTAIN COMPETENCIES

PATRICIA CROSS: Maybe learning-how-to-learn is a set of skills in managing one's resources for learning.

MARK CHEREN: Acquiring the tools a good teacher uses to plan, organize, implement, and assess a learning project or experience.

RON CERVERO: How to do program planning for yourself.

MARK CHEREN: Possessing the ability to negotiate with mentors and resource people. The ability-capacity to reflect about where you are in life—the forces in your life situation which inhibit and facilitate your learning and participation in education.

CONTROL AND INITIATIVE

MAURICE GIBBONS: The locus of control over decision making about the [learning-related] event should rest in the hands of the learner.

MALCOLM KNOWLES: Locus of initiative may be a better term.

DAI HOUNSELL: The art of learning-how-to-learn is learning to distinguish between elements which are outside of your control and those which offer some opportunities for control. It seems to me that control and self-direction are largely myths and it seems to me that what I would see as something like a competence in learning-how-to-learn would be something like recognizing that at the margins there are a few small potentialities for having some control in the situation. We like to think that somehow or other there is a situation to gain control over and mostly there isn't—even in very, very open situations. Ninety-five percent of the factors in the situation are more or less inflexible because of the context, because of your own situation, and so on.

ROBERT SMITH: Isn't it a matter of recognizing the situation? If you're going to learn Sumo wrestling in Japan and you say, "I want to develop my own program," you aren't going to last very long; you deliver yourself up for the treatment. What you have to recognize are the requirements of the educational situation and the appropriate behavior—which includes the amount of control to relinquish. Another example is when the human potential movement came along in the late sixties and seventies (sensitivity training and the like). There were some people who were able to get very little out of those events where you had to relinquish control and take risks. And they didn't usually receive the necessary preparation; so it was really a bit like a lottery.

MALCOLM KNOWLES: It's important to understand the intellectual difference between learning and being taught—and between learning-how-to-learn and learning how to be taught.

RAVINDRA DAVE: Once authoritative learning is available to you, you have the right and responsibility, not just the right but also the responsibility, to decide whether you want to have it or whether this is something you would like to postpone.

MARK CHEREN: To pose an alternative to learner locus of control and initiative, could we state that the decision making and the performance of functions are open to negotiation—that the situation is by definition a negotiable one where both decision making and the performance of functions during the learning experience are both open to negotiation? So then, in some situations it is externally directed, if you will, almost entirely; in others, more functions are controlled by the learner.

ALAN KNOX: Clearly learning-how-to-learn does not mean learning-how-to-learn all by yourself—solitary learning—so let's just rule that out. And learning-how-to-learn has much to do with being able to at least believe that you're helping to shape major decisions about what will be learned, how it will be learned, what the emphases would be, and so on. So it has to do with, in a sense, locus of control whether or not it involves some sort of negotiation. And so the full-time student at Harvard can indeed have a sense of what she's trying to accomplish in an academic department, and she can use effectively the faculty, library, and other resources while accepting what she can't change in the structure that she finds herself in; she can still be very much in control in Knowles' terms.

Boundaries

Here the principals try to move toward definition and the establishing of some outer limits for the domain of learning-how-to-learn. One person referred to it as changing focus from quintessences to boundaries. At least one feared that such inquiry might prove counter-productive.

ROBERT SMITH: I don't know about boundaries. It seems to me that we could go insane trying to establish boundaries—disputing over whether #39 should be in or out. If we had the core, the boundaries could take care of themselves for our purposes.

They began by suggesting examples of matters that seem to be "on the border of the domain." They also concerned themselves with what it "isn't," quickly agreeing that indoctrination and brainwashing were beyond the pale.

ALAN KNOX: Making people passive learners is not included.

PATRICIA CROSS: Is learning how to be taught a kind of inner limit [most limited interpretation of the concept's meaning]?

ROBERT SMITH: Learning to learn definitely involves "learning."

DAI HOUNSELL: I'd say learning does *not* qualify. It's what's left when you subtract "learning" [from the phrase].

ROBERT SMITH: Elsewhere I have suggested that I saw as kind of boundaries first of all basic skills—what we were talking about a while ago, like reading.

ALAN KNOX: That's inside, you're saying? That's inside that domain?

ROBERT SMITH: Yes. It seems to me that it certainly includes acquiring or possessing the basic skills as well as the main skills that go with collaborative, autonomous (or self-directed), and institutional learning. And then there is the information that's coming to us from Europe, where they say that what you've really got to pay attention to before you go into those procedural skills is the very nature of how the person perceives learning, knowledge, and him or herself.

You've carved out quite a big area right there. Now you get into the more debatable parts. For example, do you think we ought to spend a lot of time helping people to negotiate the institution when maybe they're in the wrong program to begin with? Maybe we ought to be changing the institutions or something. Some think a part of learning-how-to-learn is making people better consumers of education. Now it's getting bigger. People keep adding on, and I think it's a matter then of "philosophy," or almost arbitrarily saying that one sees it that way.

ALAN KNOX: It becomes very difficult to carry on a discussion if something can come from any part of the universe and be a central part of what we're discussing. So, thinking of our practical problems in these few days—trying to limit the focus of our discussion—are there any admittedly arbitrary limits?

MARK CHEREN: I've always found that most important about this is helping people to figure out where they want to go. Self-assessment and career planning are important because one's sense of purpose seems to have such a big impact on what we were trying to prepare people to be able to do. So one can say that any learning that doesn't assume that an individual has personal unique purposes should not be seen as a part of this domain.

GROUNDING THE INQUIRY

At this point the principals seemed to weary of confronting the nature and implications of learning-how-to-learn in a rather abstract manner. The need to objectify and ground the dialogue is expressed and confirmed in the following passage. The results proved quite positive in terms of motivation for the second day's inquiry and the results thereof.

DAI HOUNSELL: I think this problem of dealing with a wooly concept so generally is the obstacle to moving foreward. It seems to me that, in a sense, we're staying at a very general level while trying somehow to particularize it without sorting out what in specific form we are talking about. It seems to me that one way we can at least seek to solve the problem is to agree on something like two or three very sharply contrasting contexts and contents.

So we might think of one which takes place in a certain kind of educational setting and is very concrete and specific; and we're talking about a specific group of learners perhaps in terms of age or level or something like that (or content area). Then take another one from, say, the world of work in some sense. And maybe another one that's much more generalizable. We don't necessarily have to tie it up with a grid.

What we try to do in small groups, then, is to determine what learning-how-to-learn means in terms of that very specific context and content. After that we try to pool the understandings from those contrasting situations. So that we can start to see what a general picture might look like from those specific instances. We might well find in those three situations that matters are so different from one another that we can't group them under learning-how-to-learn.

To do this the kind of questions we've got to ask are something like these: What does learning-how-to-learn mean here? What does it entail here? The second question (one we are continually stumbling over) is: How does learning-how-to-learn here differ from simply learning well? It seems to me that a lot of people have been talking about learning well; the two can't be the same thing.

ROBERT SMITH: That's very very well put and very important. It isn't learning and it isn't learning well.

DAI HOUNSELL: Then a way of sharpening those distinctions, is to ask a question like, "What is the scope for facilitation [training]?" Not because one necessarily wants to get into very intricate discussions about strategies, but again with the idea of enabling focus.

ROGER SALJO: Well, I wanted to say exactly what Dai said. In my experience, if you have problems with definitions of this kind, it's a very good strategy, at least temporarily, to turn to concrete instances that illustrate what you mean by certain words. And then you should carefully compare instances in order to see if there is anything in common.

ROBERT SMITH: I'd like to give an example. In a course on learning-how-to-learn I ask if this is an example of learning-how-to-learn: A teacher who has heretofore used one method decides to use four or five. Usually students feel that it is an instance of learning-how-to-learn, that the teacher is expanding the repertoire of the student, as Bruce Joyce says. I then explain that I don't agree and that the difference requires looking closely at what Joyce says: it is necessary to expose them to different methods *and* then help them to see the differences and uses of methods. Why did we use method X? When would you use this method? What skills aid learning through this method? Then learning-how-to-learn is involved. Without that it's just changes in instruction, and to call it learning-how-to-learn is to sow confusion. Maybe we could get down to some instances like this.

DAI HOUNSELL: There you just made a useful distinction, enough distinction. I can see the meaning of learning-how-to-learn very clearly; but it's very difficult if you leave out concrete references.

In the next three sections learning-how-to-learn in the context of schools and colleges is discussed. The issues include the following:
> How to instill confidence and foster motivation
> The role of self-directedness
> Developing the ability to become aware of and reflect upon learning processes and tasks
> The relevance of transference
> Generic versus context-specific competencies

IN THE ELEMENTARY SCHOOL

MAURICE GIBBONS: We've developed an approach to helping children to become "experts" in a particular area (the Expert's program). I was really interested in what you were saying about using a log; we use a working journal which has three parts: ideas, action, and reflection. The three seem to work together as a really powerful sort of set. Action is planning and reporting, and this is about action and self. It is intended to act as a kind of cycle of motivation and reflection, because I think motivation is really important in all of this.

The students are encouraged to gather the best ideas about an area of interest through "attack reading"—attacking a book savagely for what you can get from it—totally for self interest, for what's valuable and retaining that essence for yourself.

Next is something that I've found people have to be taught: that they have ideas and that their ideas are ok. It sounds sort of basic, but people can go all the way through university and it may never occur to them that it's possible and ok for them to have an original idea. I make it an absolute requirement that they do. This is where they start to plan their own independent projects. This is building a resource for ideas and starting to build a resource base of one's own, then planning and reporting objectively on what happened. What did you plan to do and then what actually happened when you put it into action? What does that mean? Sit back and think about the ideas, think about what you tried, etc. What did you learn from that action? (That may be both process and content.) And then, what did you learn about yourself? What's happening to you? Because, just as in curriculum development, one of the principles that I work with is that if the developer is not developing, it's impossible to develop a new program. That the two are inseparable.

So the program is designed as much to develop the person as it is to develop the program. I think that's kind of the key. That's the reason why there's another sort of model which says "as we work on the outer action, we have to also consider that one of the unique features of working with self-directed learning is that you have to develop the inner comparable states or it will never work." So that if you want a person to set goals that are meaningful and will really be motivating (and followed through on), there has to be a sense of clarity that this is something I care about and it is *my* goal.

Most people have never set goals for themselves, in my experience. And what you do when you're asking a person to set an independent goal is to say what is your existential meaning base. That's really what you're saying. Who are you? What do you stand for? Where are you going? What does life mean? That's really what you ask even when you're setting a goal for yourself for the next six weeks. And if the individual has no clarity about who he or she "is" and "where going", a useful goal becomes almost impossible to establish.

Somebody who is going to plan has to have the confidence that the plan can be brought off. So there's a comparable inner state—if you're going to ask somebody to evaluate himself, he's going to have to have a sense of openness. And that's one of the key features that we found—that your strategies should be as concerned about developing appropriate inner states as they are for developing the outer actions. The two are in fact interactive.

So what we're doing then is teaching people to get ready—readiness. Then what we do is really teach the process through a contract. The contract is designed to contain the process. The contract includes vision, goal, plan, challenge, management, evaluation (base line excellence), demonstration, and celebration. Now a lot of that is a combination of things, but some of the strategies are as much intended to develop and maintain that inner state as to provide the other activity.

This is really a developmental process; the student is developing the ability to be self-directing—he doesn't achieve self-direction and then go and apply it. These happen together and they happen in process.

JEAN MOON: Is it fair to say that the inner state is moving toward making reflection explicit with that child?

MAURICE GIBBONS: Let's say we're asking a person to set a goal in this program, for example. One of the things we do is to help the student start to think about what's important to him. So this may lead back to all kinds of examination of previous experiences, about things that he's enjoyed; it may be looking at the dreams he has; it may be looking at the expectations around him. So we start to build up a whole body of relevant inner factors, by giving that person process experience. It's process experience to achieve some clarity.

Now when it comes to confidence, we may not ask him to sort of clarify his confidence. What we might do then is say, this is your introduction to self-directed learning and we're going to do a three month project. We start with half hour units, then hour units, with a very simple program that simply says: what do you intend to do, how do you intend to do it well, and how will you know you've done it well? And we just start with that. We're starting to develop the whole idea of intention and responsibility and reflection on it; so we start with something really short, because we know that we have to build confidence. So we're not going to ask him necessarily to process that; but we know that he can't go ahead unless he feels he can handle it. So momentum has to be constructed and maintained.

The power of this is that it is inner development. The idea of trying to objectify education is where we've been in the past. Now what this says is, that although it's important to be intentional and have all those skills, if you don't have the appropriate inner state (superstructure) the thing will collapse on itself when you're on your own. But if you've also been developing drive, determination, openness, confidence, and clarity, then you are really rolling.

IN A COLLEGE

MALCOLM KNOWLES: Alverno College in Milwaukee has probably the most elaborate program for developing skills of learning, and I'd be interested in having Jean describe how they go about that.

JEAN MOON: When a student comes into the Alverno program—a four-year liberal arts, outcome oriented program—she gets involved with general abilities (or competencies) as well as the content of an undergraduate major. There are several abilities they seek to enhance. I believe the labels are communications, problem-solving, valuing, social interaction, environment, analysis, and ability to work with contemporary world issues and problems. Those are the factors on which the process component of their assessment program focuses.

When a student goes through her outcome program, whatever content is involved in courses is also taught "toward" these abilities; they're taught in tandem and linked together. So, for example, when you're assessed in an English Literature class, you also might simultaneously be assessed for your knowledge in terms of analysis, valuing, or problem-solving. Assessments can be in the classroom or they can be external to the classroom in what's called their assessment center.

Competency acquisition is regarded as a developmental matter. Each ability has been expressed in terms of several levels and these are sequenced so that one level builds to the next. In that sense it's a process; for instance, level one might be the ability to self-assess your communication skills in relationship to speaking, writing, listening, and mathematical ability. Level two would build upon that as would level three, level four, level five and so on.

MARK CHEREN: Is the idea that by being very directive and having taught toward these abilities, one is then empowering the student to deal better with academic issues?

JEAN MOON: The idea is that once the student is empowered with the abilities, she then can transfer those abilities to a variety of contexts.

MARK CHEREN: Transfer-taught?

JEAN MOON: I think my response to that would be that transfer happens in the process; it's the abilities that are taught.

RONALD CERVERO: The research says if you don't teach for transfer, it doesn't happen. I mean basically, it's not quite that simple. I don't know exactly what we mean by transfer. You have to have something to transfer.

THE OPEN UNIVERSITY

RAVINDRA DAVE: The [United Kingdom's] Open University developed an orientation course and some little booklets and so on for new students. It's a very short program, but a study was carried out that showed significant difference between the academic performance of those who took this course and those who did not. They also discovered that learning-how-to-learn is not something that has to be taught to each and every person in the system. I think human beings have some kind of an intuitive feeling for finding their way, but a little help in a more systematic manner is likely to do some good.

DAI HOUNSELL: I'm not sure about that, because they've actually changed their approach. I was the assessor for some preparatory packages they produced, and the situation in basic terms is that someone would be formally registered and accepted for a course by about September and the foundation courses don't start until January. And so what they produced were some preparatory packages which are subject oriented—five courses that are optional for the students to work with during that period.

At the same time, I think it's very clear that the whole approach has become much much less normative than it was. The early guidebooks said something like, "You must find a clean, quiet place to study, study for a given period of time, take frequent breaks," and so on. Actually they have discovered through institutional research that some students don't work in that way at all. And so they're now much more liberal in terms of what they are doing.

PATRICIA CROSS: But is it still study tips? I would certainly call those study tips. Not learning-how-to-learn, necessarily.

DAI HOUNSELL: I don't personally see an introductory or pre-course intervention [to develop competencies in higher education institutions] as all that useful, except for a bit of consciousness raising. I think you can do much much more after a course starts, when people have got a feel for what goes on.

The other problem that I had, doing the kind of things that you've talked about, is that I began to feel that most of it was really not connected with what the students were doing in their day-to-day work. Because what I was offering was effectively a kind of general purpose course and most of the students were in subject oriented situations with very specific contexts. So a skill area like reading or problem-solving means different things in physics, economics, history or English. Most of the students thought most of the time that we weren't actually addressing things that were relevant to them.

I think that gets us back to fundamental problems: the difference, if you like, between what's universal and what's specific—the extent to which there are generic skills—and the matter of transference.

It seems to me that the relationship between the specific and the general is very very problematic and very difficult to handle. I'm not sure, for example, that even if one effectively equips a student with a whole semester in problem-solving that you necessarily equip him with anything that might help him in the first kind of problem-solving task encountered in the next term.

RONALD CERVERO: Because they have to problem-solve on a specific problem.

DAI HOUNSELL: Because they have to work out what it means in terms of the particular kind of content that they're dealing with and also within the kind of context where some of the expectations, some of the norms for how you operate are actually under the whim if you like.

PATRICIA CROSS: I was thinking of even a simple model which would be a kind of program evaluation. If you gave people three days of a course in learning-how-to-learn and you accept course grades as a criterion, then it's quite distinguishable as to whether people who took your three-day course did better or not as well in their courses. If you accept the premise which is I think at least relevant that people who learned how to learn would do better in college than those who did not, who cares whether it's a generic or specific? It's the criterion that's the problem.

DAI HOUNSELL: Yes, exactly, what are your criteria of achievement at the end of that course?

PATRICIA CROSS: It seems to me this question of whether it's generic skills—I take it you're convinced that there are some generic skills—or whether it's specific to the course is a thoroughly researchable question.

IN THE WORKPLACE

Most people have occasion to learn in and through employment settings. Organizations in the USA alone invest tens of billions of dollars in educational programs and "human resource development" activity. An appropriate role for the learning-how-to-learn concept and process in this setting received considerable attention at the conference. As mentioned earlier, it was one area of practice selected for examination by a subgroup as a way of clarifying the meaning and domain of the concept. That group first identified some instances of real or hypothetical learning-how-to-learn applications and later presented case examples to the other principals for reaction. At another session, the case examples served as the basis for a broader-gauged discussion by principals, observers, and others interested in workplace implications. Some of the latter persons possessed experience as consultants and trainers in human resource organizations.

Some of the issues and questions raised or implied in this passage include the following:

- Why human resource organizations might wish to pay attention to learning-how-to-learn. Building the case.
- Do we know enough about learning in the workplace itself to make useful applications?
- What is already being done in the way of theory-building and applications?
- What form might a useful orientation to learning-how-to-learn take?
- Learning how to cope with major changes.
- How self-directedness in learning and its enhancement might fit in.
- What are the implications of the fact that so much workplace education is embedded in work procedures and day-to-day problem solving?
- The role of HRD and training personnel in learning-how-to-learn applications.

AN INTRODUCTORY TRAINING EXPERIENCE

ROBERT SMITH: I've been trying to develop a learning-how-to-learn experience for first and second-line supervisors. It would probably take the form of a workshop. The main goals would be: (1) to foster self-understanding as learner (which I consider central in any "generic" kind of training); and (2) the acquisition of some appropriate organizing skills. The training activities would include learning style diagnosis and discussion of the results; discussion of relevant case studies; and looking closely at how learning presently goes on in the organization in question and what might further enhance it. When they came away from it the particpants would have considerably increased their insight into themselves as learners; they would also be prepared to use what Mark (Cheren) calls self-organizing skills. They'd have a bit of a basis for further activity. For example, if they're going to undertake some learning task off the job—like carrying out a personal learning project—or if there's a problem coming up in their work area and they know they've got to get busy and learn about it, how they could approach that a little more systematically than they have in the past. And also how they could be more helpful to their subordinates and peers as a facilitator or co-learner with them.

ALAN KNOX: What is there about self-understanding as a learner as a goal of such a workshop that you see as especially important and where does learning style diagnosis fit in?

ROBERT SMITH: In introducing the concept I find it useful to provide some theory and activity for taking a look at oneself as learner. Diagnosing learning style is an efficient way to trigger that. And it provides some specific labels like field dependence/independence or left-brain/right-brain.

ALAN KNOX: What would a case study look like?

ROBERT SMITH: One might describe an instance when people have to adapt to change and learn a significant new process or procedure— word processing for example. It might describe people at a workstation being upset when they discover that the organization is "going electronic." Then you could have the participants analyze what happened and think together about the implications for the next time this kind of thing occurs.

ALAN KNOX: So at least one purpose of the case study is to encourage people to reflect on past instances in which they've been engaged in learning activities, and then ask them, almost in a meta-sense, to critique, analyze, figure out what went well, what went poorly, what they've learned in that experience that is transferable to another.

CARRYING OUT A LEARNING PROJECT

MARK CHEREN: I have been trying to picture how people would be operating in organizations if learning-how-to-learn had come of age (after we had successfully run Bob Smith's workshop and perhaps many others), if learning-how-to-learn was part of the environment of the organization.

I have pictured two supervisors who both had a performance problem with one of their staff members. They discovered this one day when talking at lunch. What they discovered in talking about it was that they both had trouble confronting individuals about performance problems. They said, let's work together to do something about this. So they needed help in conducting discussions about work improvement—a standard need in the training and development field. Looking at this in stages, this represents initial, broad, needs assessment. The first thing they had discovered at lunch was they had a common problem and they described it in general terms—to learn to do a better job at talking with a staff member about how to improve what he or she is doing.

The next step is to engage organizational support. So if people really know how to learn, they might go to their supervisor—each of them has a supervisor, a manager—saying, I'd like to work on this developmental [or educational] project; another supervisor and I have talked about it and we'd like to work on it together, what do you say?

So, theoretically both of their managers say yes. So we've got two managers buying into what two first-line supervisors want to learn: how to better confront staff members about improved performance.

I'll try to talk about what seems to be different here from what usually happens. The first thing that's different is that you don't often get two supervisors who talk about a learning need and start to get this formal about it together; I don't think this is a frequent occurrence. The fact that they don't just talk about it and maybe pass the buck back and forth but they go the next step—talking with their supervisors about doing a project together starts to be where this diverges from current reality or norms. Now they have obtained organizational support.

Now they need to identify specific needed subskills and possible resource persons. They talk about it, trading stories about their own supervisors (managers). They decide that one of those managers could be useful as a planning resource—a really supportive person for differentiating the sub-skills that are involved. This already starts to be different from the norm because they have taken responsibility for differentiating the sub-skills. When was the last time you saw anybody do that at the work site? This does not usually happen but it should any time you're going to learn something new.

That's the general area of need. Now, what are the sub-parts and which ones do I want to acquire or improve? If we were training well for learning-how-to-learn, that would begin to be part of their repertoires.

So they talk to that manager about the skills and actions involved, such as giving positive and negative feedback and clarity about expectations, both important parts of a work improvement discussion. They seek to understand why the one manager is so successful at this matter. After a bit, they begin to devise a plan. Each may talk to his manager alone . . .

about what his personal strengths and limitations are in those sub-skills. Each has to figure out with his manager the priorities for the project. That again should be a normal part of a development effort: you figure it out, you come to a concensus with your supervisor about what your strengths are, what your weaknesses are, and what the priorities are—given the needs of your work unit in the next year or so and possibly in terms of your career development goals.

They negotiate those, and then they go back and start considering activity options, given their combined list of proficiencies to work on. In this case they may go outside because nothing on work improvement is being offered by their training department. Or maybe their manager tells them about another manager from whom they can get help through coaching. So again they're breaking set, doing it differently by not just going to one place for information, and coming back and using it.

And let's say that, because they have been specific about sub-skills, when they talk with another person in the organization about one matter, they learn about the importance of "cuing"—questioning phrases used in a work improvement interview; so they have identified another sub-competency with the help of this new resource person. And that person also mentions a good film called "Face to Face;" and they contact the training department about obtaining that film.

Now we've got it multi-media with three different resources, and we haven't even gotten to reading. They then start reading together and sharing things from various sources.

ROBERT SMITH: All that was kind of pre-planning, wasn't it?

MARK CHEREN: That's all pre-planning, right. But they're taking responsibility for a lot of things that professional trainers or professional educators would ordinarily do for them; and I think that's what makes this story so far qualify for a learning-how-to-learn story. It's nothing dramatic, but it is significantly different from what usually happens and would represent initiative coming from any angle—and particularly from the individual in a way that I guess we would agree is wholly desirable, preferable in this day and age.

Then they consider their options and come up with a detailed plan; they implement the plan, move along, and give each other peer support.

An important thing in this context is the practice or the application afterwards; if you haven't started using it on the job, it isn't a serious learning experience as far as I'm concerned. Then they work out with their managers an end-point where they will assess whether (or where) the performance on the job is improved according to the standards that they set at the beginning of the experience.

Now, again, a lot of this would ordinarily be done by the training department. If you went somewhere and took a course, you wouldn't get involved in several of these things; what we want is not that people will always do all of this in so much detail, but an organizational environment with these kinds of options available to each individual—one in which their supervisor or manager would feel completely comfortable in collaborating. The training department would even be set up to document a project that has variety of that sort. So it's a world that is comfortable with the kind of active learning we have been talking about.

PARTICIPANT: I'd like to comment on both illustrations— first, concerning a suggestion that it would be useful to develop the workshop only after you really understand a particular workplace. So you could put those behavioral objectives (that are going to be the outcomes of your workshop) in a manner that you could articulate them pretty clearly in terms of "my kind of work place, my kinds of materials, my kind of people."

ROBERT SMITH: Okay. And maybe the word learning is not always operative to begin with.

PARTICIPANT: It might not be; maybe a better word would be problem solving. But I could see the consultative process fitting what you are describing so well. You also need to consider objectives, jargon, communication patterns, social rewards, and punishments.

ROBERT SMITH: These are things that have to be taken into account.

PARTICIPANT: Yes, that I would want to know. Who really makes decisions about change?

PARTICIPANT: Sounds like what you're talking about is the basic culture of the organization.

PARTICIPANT: Exactly. I think you've got a great model but I think it's got to be utilized to a very high degree on a consultation basis.

ROBERT SMITH: Would you explain that a little more?

PARTICIPANT: Adapted to how the organization defines the situation, where they feel their shoe pinches. And then put it in behavioral objectives that would readily appear to have relevance for them.

PARTICIPANT: I was also thinking about your (Cheren's) illustration of a process. I wonder if we realize the extent to which HRD activity in industry today is moving toward that model. For example, a quality circle program does most of the things that you've got up there as a part of the process. And so we have some things by which we could help them implement, amplify, and the like, but there's a number of things happening in industry today that are moving in that direction—especially in the service industries, using service industries very broadly.

MARK CHEREN: I'm involved with quality circles where I work, but I don't know if people actually go so far as to make full development projects out of the needs generated by the circles—and that it gets put, let's say, in their cumulative training records.

PARTICIPANT: Oh yes. It all depends on whose quality circle model you follow; you know some models have a very detailed manual in which all of that must be done. Others call it quality circles when a group gets together and complains once a week.

ROBERT SMITH: I would like to add one thing. As long as we're picturing the ultimate, super organization of the future, then I think these people would finally sit down and say what did we learn about learning processes themselves from our collaborative experience? For the next time we encounter a problem (and decide it's an educational or learning problem, whatever you want to call it) it's going to involve our setting some objectives and getting some resources, etc. Then they would have so fully internalized the learning-how-to-learn notion that they couldn't do something like that without concluding by not only evaluating it as an educational or problem solving event but also evaluating it in terms of learning about learning itself.

MAINTAINING LEARNING SKILLS

PARTICIPANT: I'm even wondering if that side of it doesn't need to be integrated more often in other organized training procedures and programs. So that if you really want to find out how effective you are, it isn't necessarily what you get on the paper and pencil stuff concerning how well they did. So often there are problems when you take the training back to the job site and find that the transfer didn't really make it. And we don't know why it didn't happen except six months from now if you go into the site you find out that actually they're still doing it the way they did it before they came to the training session. And maybe, as trainers, that's a side of it—that maybe we need to do some informal or maybe more formal-ized evaluation (even within the delivery system), asking: "Are you understanding? How are you think-ing about this? What process did you go through to come to that conclusion? Now if you have a problem like that, what kind of steps did you use to solve it here; were there problems with that (maybe getting input from others in the group)?" You don't very often get the luxury of teaching that tightly—especially for middle management and those kinds of problem solving they do. I don't see a lot of that happening in the consultive work that I'm doing.

Robert Smith: Your mentioning of the importance of put-ting new knowledge and skill to use reminded me of the need to pre-plan for the maintaining of new behaviors. Sue Ross's study of successful weight losers showed that their success was largely a func-tion of the realism of their planning for maintenance as opposed to the initial losing of weight. And as people begin learning in new and more active ways, it will be necessary to support them in their efforts—all of which may not be highly successful.

Mark Cheren: From the point of view of the organiza-tion's training staff, I think an implication is to bring in members of the organization periodically to find out how their personal development efforts are going—to talk, to reflect, and to keep alive self-consciousness about self as learner as people con-tinue managing their own growth and development. That has to be a regular part of things if we're going to do less spoon-feeding. And that is one kind of place where you get to apply some organizational development principles—where through planning analysis and midway analysis one seeks to guard against throwing training at, for example, a structural problem.

Participant: I wanted to comment that, from a consul-tant's perspective, all those things underneath number four (on the list) are what organizational development consultants do. And so I see the role of the consultant as an important part that's missing here. It's almost as if you're framing this so that the learners are independent of any kind of facilitators or guidance. I think that the role that the consultant plays in facilitating learning is integral. Particularly because learning in an organization is in a context where there is often an imbalance of power, and the consultant usually balances power. And the second thing that is missing here is the time frame. Many of the things talked about take several (even five) years to accomplish. I think that's an integral under-standing because most people want it to happen much faster than it usually does.

SELLING THE CONCEPT

ROBERT SMITH: One might draw an analogy there with training for collaborative learning where people want to give a few hours of training in hopes that the result will be groups that can really function together and communicate and listen. There is the question of how to get people to stand still for process training (or learning-to-learn skills development) while the meter is running.

PARTICIPANT: I think the key is not to get people to stand still but to get them into the learning itself. You get them to participate and develop their own learning but the role of the consultant is really to engage them in their own learning projects.

MARK CHEREN: I was trying to posit the supervisor as hav-ing been trained as the learning consultant and . . . . but you're right, there's still going to be a role always for the expert, the real professional learning and development consultant in the organization (or office of consultants) however well we may get rank and file organization members and supervisors to take initiative for development and problem solving.

Roger Harrison used to do this for executives in a

five-day workshop called self-directed learning for executives. I'm not sure he would have prepared people for the same skills in quite the same way that we've been talking about. It is true that what I'm picturing is the time when we're training virtually everybody in the organization for making all of this sort of thing happen on a regular basis so that you don't need anything "artificial"—even a quality circle—as the excuse for it. It literally becomes "the way we all operate."

ROBERT SMITH: I might also mention, just to give us a little more framework, a couple of areas that I've seen turning up in the training and development journals. One idea that is catching on is that if you're giving an educational event—a one-day sales training workshop—it's often useful to devote the first hour or so to preparing the participants for getting the most from that event. I saw a longer example described where they were going to provide some employees with a four months' full-time course in some technical material—I think it was electronics. They devoted the entire first week to getting ready to learn. They provided training in note-taking; since they were going to be using small groups at times, they provided training in how to participate when we move into that mode—also memorization, and so on.(Carlisle, 1985)

An article called "Socialization to Learning" (Sanders and Yanouzas, 1983) provides a theoretical base for an aspect of learning-how-to-learn. It centers in the notion that when people come into an organization, if they are going to be involved in educational programs, they're eventually going to be socialized into the fact that this is the way things go on around here; for example, that you don't ask any questions when management is teaching the course. The idea is that you can prepare people in a better way than that.

And I've seen several other articles in the training literature about using learning style diagnosis not only for instructional purposes (which I wouldn't call learning-how-to-learn) but also for this purpose of helping the members of the organization to get more insight into themselves as learners.

PARTICIPANT: I was wondering if this could be broadened out beyond the non-profit organization, or is it definitely a business-centered concept that we're talking about? Also, are we talking about human resource development in terms of developing persons, or is this mainly supervisory resource development?

MARK CHEREN: I definitely meant to broaden it in both directions—to non-profit human resources development and for all staff. I used the supervisory skills merely as an example—it's definitely for all staff. In fact, that's the challenge—to equip everybody at all levels. Also, there are obviously levels of sophistication in learning-how-to-learn skills; some are metacognitive skills, for example. We're probably assuming an awful lot about where the individual is with regard to development when we speak of making everybody in an organization a skilled learner. It becomes as much a problem as it would be in getting everybody in a school system to develop the necessary awarenesses and competencies.

ROBERT SMITH: Well, dissemination is certainly going to be an uneven matter; we hold this up as a model— something to work or plot against. In a company that doesn't even stress education, it is unlikely that there would be much interest in helping people learn how to conduct personal learning projects related to productivity, let alone renewal and enrichment off-the-job. If you can sell that, you should be doing something else—like saving the world from nuclear destruction.

PARTICIPANT: Earlier you used an example of what happens when something like processing comes into an office. How would one apply this; what steps would one take when that happens?

ROBERT SMITH: Well, we know that the steps should be different from what usually happens. What usually happens is something like this. One person says, "I hear that now they're trying out one of those machines over there and soon we're going to have to learn to use it. By God, I'm not going to learn it!" That's probably the person who a year later says, "I want the machine; I love it." Now continue along the lines of the ideal learning environment (in an organization where training events would already have dealt with case studies like that). We would have been training people for the time when comparable events occur. We would have asked each work station group, "How can we organize ourselves to make them less traumatic, and (if you want to use idealistic terms) make them growth experiences rather than frightening experiences?" When the time comes then, as we've discussed, the consulting role would come in. You would probably work with sub-groups and tailor it to the different units.

MARK CHEREN: Some other suggestions might look like this: First we attempt to demystify word-processing—making it clear that there's an emotional aspect, and then doing something about demystifying it. Secondly, we ask individuals how they best learn to use machines. And then we create at least two options. One is for the people who like to go in and mess around with it for a while. Within that group there may be a sub-group of people that do it alone, and one for those who like to learn with one other person (they're kind of hand holding through it). The other people don't want anybody near them and they want blinders (at least little voting booths type of protection) so that nobody sees them. Then there may be other people who want very much to have a guide, a more experienced guide or programmed learning.

PARTICIPANT: I get lost in these big esoteric matters—I come from across the street in instructional technology.

ROBERT SMITH: Well then my answer is that we would program the whole effort.

PARTICIPANT: So I don't know about doing big workshops on learning-how-to-learn to get people to be better and approach learning situations better. It sounds great, but I think there should be more applications in existing training events. For example, as you were talking about, taking the first hour to help them understand where you're going to go with the rest. Maybe you take the first five minutes of a particular learning activity—if it requires, say, concept attainment—to prepare them (without telling them now we're going to teach how to learn a concept). Maybe applications that help people learn better need to be built right into the delivery system, study materials, preparation and so on. Those kinds of things might well be included in the needs assessment when you're identifying needed proficiencies—a part of front-end analysis. I don't see that being done as much as it might be.

INFORMAL LEARNING AND PROBLEM SOLVING

PARTICIPANT: Most of the organizations I work with do not have formal education programs, which means that the importance of informal learning increases. The grape vine and the huddles that exist are really prominent in non-profit organizations. Some guy at IBM published a book called *Huddling* [V.D. Merrell, American Management Association, 1979]. He went around asking about how people huddle, and he found that to be a very dominant pattern for learning—people getting together informally, focussing on a problem, figuring out a solution to it and then going at it. And he found that even in that system, where they have highly structured formal training, that huddles are very prominent. It's the way that people keep in touch with each other. And he started listing the kind of problems that they solved through huddles and it is phenomenal.

FEASIBLE OR A DREAM?

ROBERT SMITH: Do you people with experience think there really is much future for this concept and process in the for-profit sector? Or are we just getting carried away here—up above the cornfields at the end of winter?

PARTICIPANT: I think it's really important from the standpoint that in our business (the railroad business) we are finding less pat solutions as to the problems that we're dealing with in the deregulated environment that we're in. And consequently people have to become more responsive and flexible to those conditions. They have to be able to seek out other resources; we're finding that in our training sessions; we are teaching people how to be able to interview others to gather information from them better—which is an element of course of learning-how-to-learn. So, yes, I think as we get into more complex environments you have to possess some of these skills to be able to learn better independently.

PARTICIPANT: Let me take a railroading example. We had a recent crisis when the Alaska railroad lost a tank car filled with formaldehyde. The town of Moose Pass had to be evacuated. One of the comments I found myself making to the managers trying to deal with the problem was about the need to teach people ahead of time to learn how to analyze problems like that.

And I was at the Pendleton woolen mills in Washington last week, and I asked them how they went about the training process. They said, "Well, we have priorities and the workers are supposed to understand those priorities, and they're supposed

to adapt to them as those priorities become known."
So after I toured the mill with the managers, I said,
"Well, it seems to me your top priorities say that
you're more concerned about safety than about quality, earnings, or anything else." He said, "Yeah, that's
pretty much true." And I said, "Well I drew that conclusion because there's evidence of that in the
number of posters that are placed around." Then I
asked, "How about teaching people how to learn
about safety?" Again their response was that employees are supposed to assimilate that information.
The suggestion I made to them was teaching people
the process of learning about how to be safe in the
workplace and do that on a systematic basis and
use that as an operational base for learning more
skills. And they were receptive to that idea.

PARTICIPANT: You've probably read such books as *In
Search of Excellence* [T.J. Peters and R. Waterman.
*In Search of Excellence: Lessons from America's
Best Run Companies*, Harper, 1982] and *Corporate
Cultures* [T.E. Deal and A. Kennedy, *Corporate Cultures: The Rites and Rituals of Corporate Life*, Addison-Wesley, 1982] and noticed the degree to which
they're selling learning to learn. As more and more
companies go to project management, the project
committees try to utilize the skills we've talked about.
And as the service industries expand and individual
corporations grow—many are pretty small now—
they're going to want more and more of their managers trained in those skills. I know one very large
company that has very few education and training
people because they have trained their managers
to train. By and large, McDonald Hamburger works
that way and a number of other companies. And so
I think you are right in saying that there will be a day
in which most middle management people at least
have these implementing skills.

ALTERNATE WAYS OF LEARNING

A subgroup was formed early in the conference to consider learning-how-to-learn applications in the context of so-called non-rational or transpersonal learning (also referred to as holistic).

In the following excerpt some of the results of their conversation are described and reacted to.

> ALAN KNOX: Is there someone from that group who could say something about what you discussed as an example of a learning-to-learn application?

> DANA MAXFIELD: We considered alternate ways to learning, which in a way would cross several contexts (and be applicable)—including independent learning. Thinking of concrete situations we realized what we were doing was coming up with particular strategies that are used to access a level of consciousness that tends to speak more in metaphoric terms than in verbal/analytic terms. Some of the strategies would be things like bio-feedback, metaphoric play, meditation, guided imagery, dream interpretation, body movement, and music in the sense that it was described in *Superlearning* [Sheila Ostrander and Lynn Schroeder, Delta, 1979].

> From that we moved into identifying a process that might be involved in using this form of learning. The process that we finally came up with would begin with what we called the "readiness" stage. This is a stage where there is really a rational kind of data gathering. We used "priming the pump" as a metaphor. It involves pulling together thoughts. We talked about the occasion for using this kind of learning, for example when writing or engaging in other forms of creative expression.

> From readiness we moved into what we called the focus stage. Here you might be reframing the problem; it would involve some decision making, organizing, and so forth. Then there would be a choice of

strategy to be used to access a level of consciousness other than the rational level used up to this
point. Overriding all of this is the confidence that it
is going to work. The fourth stage would be insight,
often called the "ah ha experience." Then you do a
kind of recycling, bringing the rational back to bear
on the insight. You might repeat the fourth and fifth
stages or steps more than once as you work with
your insights in trying to put them into form.

With regard to learning-how-to-learn, you have to
start out not only with confidence but with the assumption that this is a valid way to learn. If you don't
approach it with that assumption you might as well
not go ahead. (Comment: Disbelievers need not
apply.) Exactly. Then there needs to be an understanding of the process, an understanding of what
you're trying to do. This process is a little different
from the kind of verbal/analytical type of learning
that people normally talk about. With regard to fostering awareness of strategies and teaching people
to use certain kinds of strategies, we know that it
has been done. It has been used in elementary and
secondary schools and in the work setting with rela-
xation techniques—also in higher education. Ginny
[Virginia Griffin] was sharing some applications in
graduate instruction.

RAVINDRA DAVE: Could you take one small example and
describe it to help us to understand this better?

VIRGINIA GRIFFIN: One of my colleagues, before he writes,
puts himself into a state of, or he attempts to use
what he calls receptive meditation—to help him with
a concept he's going to write about. Through this
receptive meditation he begins to get deeper meanings of the concept. It elaborates and opens out for
him, and he goes down inside, looking at it further—
instead of staying at the surface level. Then he begins to write. And that use of meditation he finds
very helpful. We talked about using other kinds of
activities to quiet the conscious mind so the subcon-

scious mind can produce what's there, after you prime the pump. You can organize a lot of things if you keep the conscious mind (left side of your brain) quiet for a bit; and that can happen through running or swimming or riding a horse or baking cookies or whatever. That's one of the strategies.

ROBERT SMITH: A dissertation that was done in Toronto on dreams—identifying thirty people who along the way have learned how to use dreams deliberately for decision making. And the study abstracted out what seems to be the essential process involved. Presumably you could train for that, if the author found the process and the paraphanalia and appropriate theory to support the process. I don't know that he ever turned it into workshops on "so you want to learn how to become a dream problem solver." But I believe the necessary data are there in the dissertation.

DAI HOUNSELL: When you mentioned that I thought of two things, one is the German dramatist Schiller who, when he was short of inspiration used to keep a box of rotting apples in his room; when he was having problems with inspiration he used to take a deep sniff. And in the film Amadeus, Mozart com-.poses at a snooker table. While composing he just lets the ball go and bounce off all the cushions and come back, almost mechanically every ten or twenty seconds. People often think that in learning or writing the only approach for success is to be sitting at a well lighted desk in a very relaxed way with no distractions.

ROBERT SMITH: Thinking about the parameters of the [learning-how-to-learn] problem that we talked about and the complexities of what we're dealing with, would you regard alternative learning (compared to say non-traditional programs or in school settings) as a relatively difficult area to deal with? I refer to making sure you're dealing with learning-how-to-learn as opposed to merely good or unusual experiences, or generally insightful moments of life, or nice changes of pace from pushing a pencil all day.

VIRGINIA GRIFFIN: I think it is trickier; you're probably right. I think people require a good experience so that they can develop the belief that it can work for them. They need awareness that they have the ability to use these strategies to produce some productive learning.

MAURICE GIBBONS: I think it's also interesting that what was originally thought of as alternative is rapidly becoming central in many cases. For instance, take visualization. People thought ten years ago, "what sort of baloney is this?" Now it's central to athletic programs and understood to be part of the pursuit of peak performance. Visualizing an excellent performance is useful in learning a manual skill and developing a set of new ideas. I think we begin to see a number of things that were originally alternative now moving toward the center.

DANA MAXFIELD: I'd like to add to what you've both said in answer to Bob Smith's question. We anticipated the question and agreed that the focusing stage is especially relevant to conceptualizing alternative learning as a domain of learning with learning-how-to-learn implications. In that stage one is clarifying purposes—focusing on what one is trying to do in accessing the nonrational—besides merely having an interesting experience. It involves knowing that if you're going to use it as a learning tool, there are strategies for going about it. I speak with some experience in the area of learning from dreams.

TOWARD A PARADIGM
OF
LEARNING-HOW-TO-LEARN

Early in the conference the principals encountered difficulty in communicating about learning-how-to-learn in
terms of the subject matter people learn, the settings in
which they learn, their orientations, and the requisite learn-
ing-related understandings and strategies for success. As
we have seen, the tactics with which this difficulty was
confronted took the form of (1) seeking to identify both
essences and boundaries of learning-how-to-learn; and
(2) looking closely at such contexts of application as community, school, and workplace. They then devoted the
major share of the final two days of deliberation to the
development of a relevant paradigm or model.

It was anticipated that such a construct might serve such
purposes as the following:

Enable "consistent conversation" about a particular
domain.
"Provide a design that we can work with over time."
Reflect "everything about learning-how-to-learn that
we've discussed, read, and written."
Provide "descriptive tools to distinguish when we're arguing about what."
"Separate the different contexts and intentions of learning-how-to-learn."

Activity directed toward building this model took several
forms: (1) an initial effort by two or three persons;
(2) explanation and discussion by all principals to verify
the potential utility of the initial version; (3) division into

57

two subgroups to flesh out the cells in the matrix that the model presents; and (4) comparison, contrast, and synthesis of the findings of the subgroups, together with discussion of post-conference utilization of the model for further theory building, research, and dissemination.

The model, or paradigm, that emerged takes the form of a grid. On the horizontal upper axis are five *domains*: formal, open, social, personal, and transcendental.

On the vertical axis are found a variety of *dimensions* relevant to each domain. The number of dimensions (and the labels assigned them) varied as the discussion unfolded. Perhaps most central in the different versions of them produced in subgroups are the following:

The nature of knowledge and knowing. What characterizes the knowledge available or potentially available in each domain? What holds it together [principles of coherence]? What characterizes it as an experience?

Evaluation. How is learning validated in the domain question? What is the role of standards? Does evaluation tend to be criterion-referenced or norm-referenced?

Dominant Required Competencies. What understandings, attitudes, and skills are especially important for successful learning in each domain?

Other dimensions identified included "appropriate contexts" (e.g., the workplace, educational institutions) and "metaphor"—a figure of speech that describes a particular domain (e.g., a file cabinet for formal learning).

The five domains and the two dimensions most relevant to the discussion that follows are shown in Table 1.

Conversation now revolves around the utility of a five domain construct and appropriate labels for each domain.

ASSESSING A FRAMEWORK'S POTENTIAL

MAURICE GIBBONS: A few of us have been trying to put together some of the differences and distinctions

TABLE 1. FIVE DOMAINS AND TWO DIMENSIONS

DOMAINS

DIMENSIONS	FORMAL	OPEN	SOCIAL	PERSONAL	TRANSCENDENTAL
	Closed-academic	Open-academic	Collaborative	Independent	Alternative personal
NATURE OF KNOWLEDGE AND KNOWING	Publically mediated Packaged and relatively fixed	Publically and individually mediated	Group mediated	Individually mediated Subjective Arbitrary	Mediated by self and higher self Non-rational
OUTCOMES	Mastery of a discrete body of knowledge to a specified level of performance	Similar to "formal" but often with greater enhancement of metacognitive skills	Not pre-specified. Consensually arrived at and confirmed	What is personally held true and valued	Integration Connectedness Inner and global peace

that seem to have been arising among us and trying to describe them in the form of some kind of model. We have the shadowy outlines of that now—perhaps enough to start to make some distinctions. I'd like to introduce it, if Phil Candy will permit me—just to see if it does address the knowledge gap and some of the distinctions that seem to have been bounding back and forth amongst us. It's a beginning that I think starts to move toward descriptive tools to distinguish when we are arguing about what.

ROBERT SMITH: How did you label it?

MAURICE GIBBONS: A paradigm that separates out the different contexts and intentions of learning-how-to-learn.

ALAN KNOX: And that might then be useful for focusing on some of the gaps in knowledge about learning-how-to-learn. We can draw in some of what we know already and what might be added.

MAURICE GIBBONS: Yes, I think we could sketch it out fairly quickly so people can see whether it's a useful direction or not.

PHILIP CANDY: When we went away yesterday afternoon, our intention was to draw a diagram which summarized everything that everybody has ever said on this subject on one piece of paper. And we began drawing circles and then we found that they weren't three-dimensional enough; and then we began drawing boxes and they didn't work; and then we began drawing things that did this and that—kind of went off the page. And the more we talked about it the more we felt that one useful approach to understanding it was the various sorts of epistimological bases of knowledge that have their impact, that are found in the notion of learning to learn different kinds of subject matter. And I guess, provisionally, we said, well let's run with Habermas' distinction between practical knowledge, communicative knowledge and emancipating knowledge just as a sort of quick rubric. We've since sort of revised it slightly and said that one kind of knowledge is well known to all of us. To use Bernstein's terms, it's got strong framing and strong classification. That is, the boundaries of the knowledge are clearly delineated: history is different from French, and French is different from mathematics, and mathematics is different from physics. It's got clear limits and it's got clear framing. It's divided into boundried mental mouthfuls that people have to acquire; it's cumulative; and there are public criteria for success, for progressing through. And that's the kind of thing that universities and schools and colleges tend to deal in, at least the predominant thing is closed, formal, academic knowledge based.

MAURICE GIBBONS: One of the things that we're attempting to do with this is to identify, almost in the form of domains, the separate areas in which we heard people talking about learning-how-to-learn. Because it seemed that we were overlapping. One of us would talk about one domain and then another would talk about the other domain, and, of course, the conditions, the strategies, the orientation, the subject matter, etc., were different in each case. So this is an attempt to sort out the orientations or domains so that we can look at them as distinctive, almost as bodies of knowledge (but we're not sure that will hold) that have their own descriptive, intrinsic nature, and therefore their own patterns of internal characteristics.

We're not saying that when learning-how-to-learn occurs it's got to occur in one of these five ways—they can be mixed; you can have a mix of all five; but when we mix them we are also mixing orientations and mixing perspectives and mixing rules, etc. So what we've done is the typical germanic classification exercise of sorting out so that we can talk consistently about a particular area. And the whole exercise now is to start to fill out those domains. So, as

Phil [Candy] is outlining here, our first attempt, it is important to try to see if we have potential with this construct. And if not, what other categories do we need; what do we need to collapse, expand, rename or whatever? Because all that influences how we go ahead and any assumption that we've got a solid working framework that we can fill out. This then is the framing we're proposing to give purpose and focus to our deliberations.

ALAN KNOX: It would appear that the first two of those parallel very much Bob [Smith]'s "institutional" category, and the third what he calls collaborative learning [in *Learning-How-to-Learn*, 1982]. And so there seems to be a nice parallel.

MAURICE GIBBONS: We've really tried to pick up everything that we heard here. It's not a sense of this is what we believe; it's a sense of trying to reflect everything we've heard and some of the other things we've read and brought out.

ROBERT SMITH: What's the second item in the left hand column?

MAURICE GIBBONS: This is a wonderful phrase of Roger Säljö's, "distinctive constellations of competencies."

PHILIP CANDY: The socially negotiated we saw as arising out of, for the most part taking place within group context, where a group of people work together or who have some shared interest come together to learn, to create ways of pushing forward some common project and where the need for learning arises out of that. Now some of the learning they might need to do may well be discipline-based learning. But if, for instance, they were observing their own processes, if they were learning how to get on well together, the kind of thing that happens in organizations, then there's a distinctive form of knowledge that has to do with communicative competence and interpersonal relationships and so on.

MAURICE GIBBONS: I'll just go back to the "Open" category and outline that a bit. We thought about the distinction (and we think it's a really important distinction) between the formal, what we call closed, and the more open approach to academic learning. What we conceived of as the open form would be to say something like this: How would formal knowledge be dealt with if it were dealt with for purposes of learning-how-to-learn? And that's what we consider to be the opposite, if you like, or the distinction between it and the formal knowledge in which authorities gather together and construct the knowledge most worth teaching directly to students in some structured way.

PATRICIA CROSS: Is there any present model of that?

DAI HOUNSELL: Yes, there is.

MAURICE GIBBONS: We're not sure that there is. Are you thinking of the Open University?

DAI HOUNSELL: No, I'm thinking of what we call something like independent studies.

MAURICE GIBBONS: No, it's not it. This will be an interesting distinction because in that, the bodies of knowledge are still thick but the approach is different.

DAI HOUNSELL: This is the situation: you work within a formal academic institution, and you have to effectively design your own course unit. And you have to form a coherent major. You negotiate those with faculty, and so effectively you design your own curriculum; and you also negotiate how you're going to be doing it.

MAURICE GIBBONS: That's very much like Antioch University.

OTHERS: Or Empire State, or external degrees, or contract majors.

PHILIP CANDY: I'm not sure that we caught the spirit of this because I'm talking here about different kinds of knowledge and you're talking about different ways in which to acquire knowledge.

MAURICE GIBBONS: Let me see if I can describe my perspective on it. How would you structure the world of knowledge if it were being structured for people to learn how to learn? It would start with the sense of, what is the domain of knowledge, what are the modes of inquiry? What would be the first principle of learning, would be the modes of inquiry, of generating knowledge within that field, etc.? So that if a person learned that, they would be empowered to learn how to learn about that field and within that field. What are the processes that are employed? What are the broad structures? What are the skills, etc.? Not starting with the content; the content would be generated as it is relevant to the issues which are the major issues of that field. So that as the person learned that field, what they were learning would be inseparable from learning how to learn. I suppose if physics was in fact the field, they would be learning to be physicists.

ROBERT SMITH: Well, isn't that what happens when one of our week-end colleges or a university such as Wisconsin-Oshkosh sets up a new way of looking at the body of knowledge for a baccalaureate? They leave out a lot of traditional material, and they may even add some. So that in a sense they almost tailor a whole new baccalaureate because all the students allowed in this program are so-called mature adults who agree to learn on weekends for four years. Would that be an example?

PHILIP CANDY: If part of the program consisted of sort of taking a step back and looking at the basis of the knowledge in that field. (Smith: Only if there's a meta process.) When we coined this I was thinking of teaching people skills like self-reflection. There's a paradox in this.

ROBERT SMITH: If they could explain to the guy down the block how their curriculum differed from the regular curriculum, they would, in a sense, have been somewhat empowered to make their way around the jungle of higher education after they left the program.

PHILIP CANDY: Yes, right. In a way, it's encouraging people to have the skills to do that; skills of critical inquiry, skills of reflectivity, and so on. These are kind of publicly available skills but they are not sequentially organized or closed off in the way that the knowledge is in the first category.

MARK CHEREN: Southern Illinois University is organized in that way so that physicians in training, medical students, are going through a process that is identical to what they will go through later on as physicians, as opposed to going through traditional academic processes. You would call that "open academic." It's also what faculty experience themselves theoretically, right? That also would qualify as open academic. That is what the physicist and so on does.

ROBERT SMITH: You mean when a faculty member invents a new course?

MARK CHEREN: Yes. Or does research in an area and invents new knowledge which then gets published.

PHILIP CANDY: If you take Ronald Gross' book about independent scholarship, you find descriptions of people who, on their own initiative, without any formal or institutional affiliation, actually push out the boundaries of knowledge in some field [The Independent Scholar's Handbook, Addison-Wesley, 1982]. I mean we want to be careful of saying that the only way to acquire this kind of knowledge is in a particular context.

MAURICE GIBBONS: The distinctive feature is that in the "formal", the knowledge is fixed as a body in all its dimensions and then is taught by the teacher.

ROBERT SMITH: The Koran might be an example.

MAURICE GIBBONS: Yes, it would be a great example. But the canons of formal of physics, the physics which is taught in schools (which is usually a paradigm shift behind) is another good example. It doesn't matter how that is taught, it's still taught as the knowledge that you will all learn, and we, as the authorities, will find the best way for you to learn it.

DAI HOUNSELL: Right, and the distinction here [with the Open domain] is one that says, we are looking together at this body of knowledge to find the ways that will be most empowering to you to become involved in it—to have the appropriate background and necessary skills and to be involved in a continuing way, working with the issues that are fundamental to this field.

PHILIP CANDY: I wonder if we can look at it this way: with the "Formal" what happens is that knowledge remains fixed and the students move through it; whereas with the "Open" the students remain fixed and the knowledge moves through them.

MAURICE GIBBONS: As long as you don't push that metaphor too far.

VIRGINIA GRIFFIN: Experiential learning has many different interpretations, of course, but one of them fits here— in which knowledge is generated by the students who may be tested against what's done. And also what's talked about by [D.A.] Schön in *The Reflective Practitioner* [Basic Books, 1983] is another example.

MAURICE GIBBONS: The thing we really have to be careful about here is seeing the approach as a distinguishing feature of this domain. It is the substance and the intent that are the distinguishing features. (Smith: Do you mean someone has finally separated content and process?) No, it's just that the way you teach it is not necessarily a defining factor in the distinction between the Open and Formal categories. We think that one of the problems we've had in our discussing is to keep mistaking changing teaching technique with changing domains of knowledge and orientations.

MARK CHEREN: But then I would be tempted to over

simplify and say "open academic" is a category where knowledge is still happening, being created, growing.

VIRGINIA GRIFFIN: As long as that doesn't imply that it's eventually going to be closed as soon as everybody gets around to it.

DAI HOUNSELL: I'm still trying to work out on what basis you were uneasy about excluding what we [in Britain] call independent study.

MAURICE GIBBONS: I was only initially uneasy because independent study in a number of North American books is the independent approach to the packaged learning. That was how it was initially used in some of the first books. Once you clarified it, I had no problem.

DAI HOUNSELL: Right, it's more than that, because you may not actually be creating knowledge in the sense of doing fundamental research, but you'll be carving out a new topic area by pulling together disparate knowledge from the whole.

MAURICE GIBBONS: Yes. I also think the distinction between content focus and process focus is a useful sort of kind shorthand.

PHILIP CANDY: This is obviously just an unfinished thought, what we've got here. One approach might be to put different kinds of teaching situations or learning situations on the other axis. So you would do independent study and say, well you can learn this kind of knowledge by going through formal approaches. There may be some cells [of the model] that are simply blocked off; there may be others that have got potential which isn't being explored at the moment. So, for instance, personal learning doesn't only occur in situations of self-teaching; there can be personally valued learning in all kinds of environments.

MAURICE GIBBONS: One of the ways we were thinking about this was that they could each be taken separately and seen as portals. That is, the learner can enter these in any way he likes; that is, he can come in it this way and then spread out to the others, or continue this way. And the useful thing is that it helps separate out those choices. And how they can be mixed together. So these can be considered not only domains but portals to learning itself or to learning-how-to-learn.

PATRICIA CROSS: Would you define personal [one of the five domains]?

PHILIP CANDY: I understand personally valued learning as insights which are sometimes tacit and sometimes conscious, but which are not necessarily publically shared.

MAURICE GIBBONS: It's the idea that the knowledge is whatever is studied; it is essentially selected and chosen as relative to the individual, by the individual. It may include formal knowledge, it may include something completely original and formed by the individual such as Gross's independent scholars did.

PATRICIA CROSS: Well it's kind of close to "Open Academic."

MAURICE GIBBONS: That would be fine except that we have to be able to distinguish those completely non-institutional things. And we would say then, when, let's say, open academic is treated that way, it's introducing a very personal sort of approach to that material. Because it could also be taught in a very formal way—as it is even in some business and law programs.

DAI HOUNSELL: To relate this to Phil Candy's personal example of his study of geneology, he might feel satisfaction in terms of his geneological quest when he reaches the stage where he feels he can trace his roots. And in an open learning situation the outcome would perhaps have to be a less personal one in which one has to conform to external standards even if there are some possibilities to negotiate.

MARK CHEREN: As you describe "open academic," and we come back to it, it sounds like it's the process of knowledge creation or knowledge as a process or as a discovery process. Trying to call it a body of knowledge has the difficulty that you're also trying to get us to accept that it is an on-going process. Virginia [Griffin] seems to insist that it be qualified that way, and she's right; so that's what we're struggling with—talking about knowledge creation as a process in "open academic" and allowing people to be part of that process, as opposed to this other [i.e. "Formal"] static notion of what knowledge is.

DAI HOUNSELL: With open academic, what you arrive at still has to conform to some kind of academic standard. That's what seems to me fundamental, because you've got the openness in terms of what you decide is effectively the curriculum (which in a sense you may be constructing at the time), but we still have to conform to academic standards. What makes it more complicated is that you may be also trying to change those norms and standards themselves. And if we take some area like ethnographic qualitative research, you've got a situation where, in a sense, new knowledge is being created, and you also have to somehow or other get the norms changed for what counts as rigorous work in order to have validity.

MAURICE GIBBONS: Even if we're doing physics, within this framework there's still all the, let's say processes that are involved; there are the basic concepts that have been generated, the paradigms; there's a body of knowledge and history that's relevant; but the difference is that these would be learned and identified even with much more participation by the student. And the approach would be through the process of creating physics. The idea is not "what'll we do in physics today?"

ALAN KNOX: The balance between the personal and the public is a useful idea for me; I find it difficult to imagine very many instances in which the learner wouldn't or shouldn't be concerned with both the personal meaning and understanding and the public standard, structure, etc. There may be a few, but even in the "alternative," it seems to me, we come back again to some basis of relating, understanding, validating, etc.

DAI HOUNSELL: So there is an issue here which has to do with something like what we consider to be a kind of focal concern—Roger [Säljö]'s distinction between what's foreground and what's background. In a good formal academic program as well as in an open academic program, you would hope or perhaps expect there'd be some kind of personal growth and development. But if we move along to the personal domain, then personal growth, self-development, is absolutely the core and comes to center stage.

ALAN KNOX: What I'm trying to get away from is the notion that in the formal academic, the learner is completely passive, a victim, and has to fit into the machine no matter how he or she is ground up, while in the "personal" and the "alternative", you're just tripping lightly through whatever you want—being unconcerned with how anybody else ever thought about or dealt with any of the issues before. And it seems to me that those are fanciful extremes; I can conceive of so few instances in which those extremes would apply that the notion of some sort of reasonable balance seems appropriate.

VIRGINIA GRIFFIN: I'm wondering if "alternative" is something we ought to find another word for. I'm not sure that transpersonal would do it, but that's one that comes to mind and comes closer. "Alternative" leaves it open. And Bob [Smith] included in his book under "alternative" a lot of things that I would think fall under one of the other four categories.

MAURICE GIBBONS: There's a question as to whether we've distinguished usefully between what is normally personal and what is transpersonal. It seemed to me that there was something superordinate about this (something in which the person looked outside himself or herself) that seemed to be usefully distinctive and that there's no problem—just as we can collapse all these elements into a single program and see their particular relationships. The question is whether or not it's a useful distinction.

ALAN KNOX: Leaving aside the label question, I'm inclined to keep all five categories separate until we look at distinctive features. I'd aggregate only after there's good reason to do so.

ROBERT SMITH: As for labels, I like "alternative" because it subsumes transpersonal and some other things we haven't dealt with.

MAURICE GIBBONS: There's no question that TV, computers, movies, video disks, etc., are powerful parts of alternative learning, but the question is whether or not they're potentially powerful in all of the different domains.

OBSERVER: May I ask a question about the "personal" category? Is it intrapersonal or interpersonal?

MAURICE GIBBONS: The "social" category is the interpersonal realm. And intrapersonal would come into play in several domains.

ALAN KNOX: In the socially negotiated (or collaborative) category other people are in a sense a part of your caravan through the learning episodes. They are involved in planning it, conducting it, and evaluating it. Whereas in the independent or personal you may at certain spots reach out and involve other people, but you are the main traveller, the person with continuity all the way through.

MAURICE GIBBONS: Have we agreed that these five categories are useful and should remain distinctive from each other, at least until we test them further? (Agreement)

PHILIP CANDY: What have we said about the relationship between personal and alternative? My feeling is that I'd like to see them subsumed under a single heading.

MAURICE GIBBONS: Does anyone want to try to summarize those two distinctions?

ALAN KNOX: I think that as with closed academic and open academic, there's a lot of similarity. In practice there is probably a continuum. But it's useful to maintain those distinctions until we have tested the model sufficiently to discover whether in fact there is enough differentiation to warrant keeping them separate.

PHILIP CANDY: There is no alternative understanding which isn't personal, so I would be inclined to put personal across the top and then to distinguish between conscious and pre-conscious (or tacit or transpersonal). Personal knowledge is the thing that really grabs my interest and has done so for years. It's sort of the way I've explained the world to myself; it's the system of constructs that I've built up as a result of my experience that allows me to navigate my way through the world that tells me (whether it's objectively accurate or not) why people behave the way they do, what they think of me, what's going to happen next. It's what allows me to anticipate events and distinguish one thing from another. Have any of you read Kelly's *Psychology of Personal Constructs* or works of any of his followers like Thomas and Harri-Augstein? The explanatory system that I have built up is a funny admixture of objectively verifiable things, and the mix is just as important and valid to me as things that other people would agree with. (Things like family jokes?) Yes, exactly. Much of my behavior as a teacher or as a learner depends on all kinds of myths that I feel about myself, or beliefs about the role of teacher and learner. If I were in therapy, people might start saying, well you know this is a dysfunctional way of viewing the world.

Some therapists might try to take me back to find why it's there and some might simply try to obliterate it through indoctrination or whatever. Still others try to help one raise it up to a level of consciousness and see why it's dysfunctional.

ALAN KNOX: That way of thinking about personal knowledge seems to apply to all five of those categories; and it seems to me that the fourth category [personal] has more to do with individually guided learning activities in which personal knowledge is an important feature; but personal knowledge also probably goes underground in the context of closed academic—where it's not valued publicly. Also, in all instances, it functions because that's the only way we perceive.

DAI HOUNSELL: It seems to me that there is a kind of knowledge which we effectively deploy or draw on all the time in professional situations, whether academics or scientists, or professionals. It's not very acessible and it's all those things that we tend to call something like craft and know-how. And actually you can't do academic work if you haven't got the knowledge. But we can't talk about it very easily. You can't actually bring it out and focus it.

PHILIP CANDY: But Habermas talks about the tacit knowledge; he argues that we know more than we can say.

MAURICE GIBBONS: And that all knowledge is ultimately personal.

PHILIP CANDY: Yes, that's a given. The other thing is Schön's notion of theory, of practice, what does he call it? Knowledge in practice, epistimology of practice, knowledge in use. I think that you'll find that personal knowledge actually overarches all these things.

MARK CHEREN: Are you saying, then, that workplace learning can go on both in the socially negotiated and interpersonal parts? And borrow from the academic pieces? I'm curious as to why we found it necessary to use the word academic here.

PHILIP CANDY: Would you be happy with [the phrase] knowledge? Technical knowledge, public knowledge?

DAI HOUNSELL: If you go outside the academic realm there are manuals for engineers, for example.

ROBERT SMITH: General Motors has a university (degree granting).

PHILIP CANDY: Xerox has a university too; they encourage copying.

MAURICE GIBBONS: If I understand the recent discussion, it is that we'll stay with personal knowledge, keeping in mind that in a sense, we're dealing with a tautology since all knowledge is personal and all that's personal can potentially be knowledge; but that we are making a distinction between the organization of the knowledge and the orientation of authority and so on.

TESTING THE FRAMEWORK

In the following section (pp.) discussion revolves around the experience of subgroups in seeking to fill in some of the cells of the model. The *Nature of Knowledge* dimension is considered first followed by the *Outcomes* dimension.

DAI HOUNSELL: what we did was tackle this problem of knowledge and knowing, a difficult matter to grapple with; we actually ended up generating a lot of buzz words that are now on paper elsewhere. We ended up by dividing the labor. We did it like a crossword puzzle, two or three person subgroups just took a column down and a line across. I can't remember who did what. I know Roger [Säljö] and I did "formal" down and "outcomes" across. So what in fact we've got sometimes in those boxes are just the thoughts of a couple of people.

ALAN KNOX: It would help me if someone were to go across those five domains, across a row, and comment briefly on why they're there (not to get into any extended discussion of those that are there).

Dai [Hounsell] do you see any particular row across that would be helpful to start with? Ok, let's see how that goes for a few minutes.

DAI HOUNSELL: Well, there's a lot more in that top row [knowledge and knowing] as I say. I think with a matrix, in the end, what you want to aim for is something that's very concise and reasonably specific. With regard to mediation, "formal," it is publicly mediated; under "open" it's publicly *and* individually mediated; under "social" it's group mediated in that the particular group establishes a frame of reference as far as knowledge is concerned. With "personal" it's individually mediated and there we also find terms like subjectivity, idiosyncratic arbitrating, and self-reference. And then the "transcendental" is mediated both by self and a higher self.

ALAN KNOX: Can we say that our emphasis with this matrix is to have a way of differentiating those people who have learned how to learn and those who have not? Then people who have learned how to learn in any or all of those domains recognize that the way of mediating knowledge is a very important aspect of what they're trying to do and that it's done somewhat differently across those domains?

DAI HOUNSELL: Yes. And I would say that when someone who has had a lot of experience in one domain considers a shift to another, he or she would be able to realize the almost revolutionary nature of what perhaps they're undergoing. For example, with the "personal" domain that you're, if you like, the individual arbiter of what counts as knowledge. And then you move into say formal academic work or even a group situation where there is involved an enormous amount of compromise. In some cases there's virtually no scope for negotiation at all about what counts as knowledge. And you realize how many problems somebody has who's a very successful learner in a personal, informal setting may encounter in a more formal setting.

ALAN KNOX: We've all had the experience of being in collaborative learning, a social learning situation, and finding at least one person in the group so locked into the personal that it was a matter of trying to get everybody else to go along, or so locked into the formal that he kept saying, "I want somebody to provide structure so we don't have to undergo any more messy negotiating."

ROBERT SMITH: And if you take it to the training level you can have a wild time trying to teach collaborative learning to a group of physicians.

DAI HOUNSELL: Academics usually can't cooperate with one another. This group is an exception of course. It's what I'm told is sometimes called the lone ranger syndrome. And moving from the "formal" to the "open academic," I don't know about the American system, but I think there's a sort of sense to the British system that the student with a first class honors degree who has done outstandingly well often is not very good at research. Research requires something that's closer to the open domain since it puts more emphasis on individual construction.

ALAN KNOX: That provides an operational definition of trained incapacity.

ROBERT SMITH: Working out a student's dissertation is a real exercise in negotiation, collaboration, with both parties learning at the same time.

DAI HOUNSELL: In its ideal form, yes. Although I think in the British context we've got everything from the old fashioned model: you find yourself a mentor and he or she tells you what to do and then you go ahead and do it. There really isn't much discussion about conceptual framework, focus, modes of inquiry or anything else. It's often a situation in which you're really kind of on your own.

ALAN KNOX: One of the by-products of the last few days seems to me is an appreciation of the range of ways of handling learning-how-to-learn in different domains, in contrast with stereotypes of what must occur or what usually occurs in any one domain.

DAI HOUNSELL: The framework gets more and more rich every time I look at it; but if you take something like the dissertation or the thesis [in Britain], we've had all sorts of problems lately which have been brought to national concern about the declining completion rates for doctorates—even among people who have had three or four-year fulltime fellowships. Funding has practically been withdrawn from certain institutions because completion rates have been below 18 percent. The causes are complex, but one factor, I think, is a kind of mix up between open and personal domains. Because, for the student, the advanced degree becomes a kind of personal quest and it has to be that in some sense. At the same time, you're supposed to get it done in three years and in a certain kind of way. If you haven't got the freedom and the openness over things like deadlines and norms and so on, it becomes a personal situation. I don't think people appreciate the discipline required.

ALAN KNOX: Yet I can think easily of instances in which advisees over the last twenty-five years have been functioning in at least the first four of our domains in terms of the way in which they were approaching their dissertations. And I think of several recent instances in which I and the institution had a great deal of difficulty. The student was probably functioning in the transcendental mode and the rest of us didn't appreciate that. Any other comments about the first row? That was helpful—to me anyway. Perhaps you could pick another row across and explain it (see Table 1).

The discussion now turns to the Outcomes dimension of the model.

DAI HOUNSELL: Let me talk about this issue of outcomes. I found it (for me) surprising that the outcome for formal learning was exactly the same in each case, which is [the] mastering of a discreet body of knowledge and skills (that are confined to a specified level). I had started with the notion that outcomes were going to be rather different—very maddening. But, if you take the whole framework as a kind of metaphor, it seems to me if it's going to be a good one, it's got to go on surprising you.

MARK CHEREN: In the example [by Alan Knox] last night, it was said that in the open situation the second major outcome is that the students continue operating to get the new knowledge—to literally build the skills and the habit and the propensity; now I don't know whether we can prove that by research (as is being tried). But there really is a difference in outcome; part of the outcome is the meta-level we're talking about. A purposeful outcome for both the learner and the educator in that open domain.

RAVINDRA DAVE: The learning-to-learn process under the "open" suggests that there are certain concommitant outcomes accompanying the main outcome. One might speculate that one outcome may be gaining greater confidence in the process of acquiring knowledge and skill (compared to outcomes in the "formal," where there may be the undesireable outcome of developing more dependence on institutional structures, for example).

DAI HOUNSELL: I think that we have to accept that. In a sense it was so big that we tried to identify the core.

ROBERT SMITH: Are you saying that if I go through an "open" program that I automatically acquire greater confidence (than in "formal") in my ability to acquire knowledge? I don't buy this. I could go through the Open University, for example, and have nothing [much in the way of meta-learning] wash off on me. It should be "processed" with the result that I get insight from the experience.

ALAN KNOX: And Howard Barrows says it's deliberate, not left to chance; it is built into feed-back mechanisms and standards. It involves encouraging medical school students to make decisions about the learning process and the strategies that they want to use—putting the burden of responsibility on them to decide how best to move from where they are to the performance of the expert diagnostician.

MARK CHEREN: Some open colleges do in fact ask that same thing—about processes and structures.

ALAN KNOX: As you know, that particular effort started at McMasters University where Barrows was before going to Southern Illinois University.

DAI HOUNSELL: The Open University concept is an interesting one because if you proceed according to a fairly tough timetable and you start from scratch, it takes six years for an ordinary degree and eight years for an honors degree. Talking to people at the Open University, one learns that, according to the institutional research, a lot of students get much much more reproductive and much more instrumental in making use of the course. I don't think that's necessarily due to the course as such; but what we've got on the one hand is a kind of a sort of life plan orientation and concern with meaning, and personal knowledge and growth. That's intersecting with the feeling that the entire degree process is taking much too long and that one is willing to do most anything to get finished. So there are those two competing interests, and I don't think you could somehow or other resolve that.

ALAN KNOX: Perhaps it would be helpful to go completely across the row.

ROBERT SMITH: May I make a comment about the process we went through yesterday in the other group. We found sometimes in filling in a cell that trying to reduce it to one dominant theme would almost distort it.

DAI HOUNSELL: I suppose mentally you have a notion that the framework ultimately becomes discussed, and these are kind of labels. I always feel when I open a book at a particular stage and there is a massive chart that the more discreet and terse the entries are, the better for digesting it. A question I think with things like this learning to learn situation is, "What is the outcome?" Is it for us or for other people?

Well, turning to outcomes of the "social" [domain], a key thing that we thought about was that the outcome was not pre-specified. In fact, a lot of the processes used are about deciding what the outcome might be, and the criteria for the outcome.

ROBERT SMITH: A lot of the learning is in the planning as opposed to the conducting of it.

DAI HOUNSELL: Right. And as we're doing here [at this conference] if you like deciding what the goal and the product of the group might be while the group is also engaged in working on some kind of kind of outcome. And then of course the issue, something that's consensually arrived at and confirmed through this process of negotiation and so one.

Under personal we've put Roger Säljö's phrase "What's True and Valued." Getting across the notion of what matters in terms of the outcome is meaning and value for the individual, and the notion that that has to do with some kind of personal truth as well as something that's valued.

DAI HOUNSELL: Turning to "transcendental," I don't know if this is a cop out. It wasn't meant to be facetious. We had real problems here, as academics, and so we came up with greater oneness" as a way of thinking about it. I don't know whether that is too global. It seems to me that if one gets into the transcendental box one has almost got to be metaphoric—if these experiences are in a sense beyond reason.

ALAN KNOX: And the phrases that are in red tend to give some sense of that as well.

DAI HOUNSELL: Yes, that's interesting because these phrases come from a different source, which is Ginny Griffin and Dana Maxfield.

MAURICE GIBBONS: Inside, enhanced creativity, connectedness, peace, inner and global peace, enhanced performance as outcomes of having learned how to learn.

VIRGINIA GRIFFIN: We also identified some negative ones which I didn't write up there. And your phrase that the open domain for some people seems to have become a way of life almost. This one can be very seductive and become a way of life for some people too. We hope that nobody does that when they become acquainted with it. We used this system to think about the balancing, being able to function in the other columns when it's appropriate and not just rely on one.

DANA MAXFIELD: If the balance is not kept, you can actually have the opposite outcome—a kind of separation and disintegration.

ROBERT SMITH: So maybe you need training for that too.
DANA MAXFIELD: I think so.

DAI HOUNSELL: One more comment. When our group got to the metaphor box we observed that schools become a kind of metaphor for itself. So we had to come up with this word bulemia, which I think has to do with vomiting. (Laughter)

VIRGINIA GRIFFIN: I was interested in Phil Candy's metaphor for the transpersonal "putting the heart before the course."

ALAN KNOX: Any other comments before we move to similar comments from the second group?

THE CENTRALITY OF COMPETENCIES

Skills for success in learning and education-related activity are often assumed to be at the heart of learning-how-to-learn. Many of the publications found in the conference bibliography make this assumption. (See, for example, Knowles, 1975; Cell, 1984; Smith, 1982 and 1983).

The organizers of the first international conference also made this assumption. The pre-conference agenda referred to core competencies for life-long learning (see page). The orientation session offered daily to the public was structured around an "organizer" based on seventeen competencies in three areas: (1) skills (e.g. academic success related skills; self-management related); (2) attitudes (e.g. inquisitiveness); (3) understandings (e.g. of the role personal assumptions about the nature of knowledge and learning).

In the early stages of their conversations the principals exhibited uneasiness about this matter but did identify learner competencies (or proficiencies) as one of the essences of learning-to-learn. As they moved through case examples and contextual applications to a paradigm of the domain of learning-how-to-learn, they found it useful to include a set of competencies as one of the major interactive components of that construct. Those competencies were stated as follows:

COMPETENCIES

    I. Cognitive Skills
      A. Understanding the Nature of Knowledge
      B. Organizing Learning Activities
      C. Critical Skills of Evaluation
      D. Thinking Convergently, Divergently, Critically, and Intuitively
      E. Retaining and Recalling Information
      F. Relating and Organizing New Information
      G. Basic Skills (reading, writing, computing)
      H. Problem Solving
      I. Understanding the Feasibility and Usefulness of Learning-How-to-Learn or Learning Process Consciousness
      J. Transference of Learning Skills

K. Communications
  1. Active listening
  2. Viewing
L. Resource Availability and Assessment (Knowledge About)
M. Organizing Learning/Development Activities
N. Cognitive Map of the Difference Between Learning and Being Taught

II. Personal Understanding
  A. Understanding of Self as Learner
    1. Preferred styles and adaptations
    2. Personal resources inventory (assessment)
    3. Personal learning awareness and monitoring
  B. Needs Assessment/Self-Assessment
    1. Sense of direction
    2. Sense of purpose
    3. Life planning
    4. Ability to find/create/generate resources
  C. Confidence, Persistence, Openness, Flexibility

III. Interpersonal
  A. Resource Accessing and Evaluating
  B. Giving and Receiving Feedback
    1. Seeking non-defensively
    2. Seeking important feedback
    3. Analyze feedback
    4. Give feedback when needed
  C. Contextual Analysis
  D. Collaborative Inquiry
  E. Using Resources
    1. Effective use of expert support
    2. Effective use of peer support
    3. Effective use of media

After the model began to take shape, a group began assigning these competencies to the five domains as shown in Table 2.

TABLE 2. FIVE DOMAINS AND FIVE DIMENSIONS WITH KEY COMPETENCIES

DIMENSIONS	DOMAINS				
	FORMAL	**OPEN**	**SOCIAL**	**PERSONAL**	**TRANSCENDENTAL**
NATURE OF KNOWLEDGE	Critical acceptance External	Critical engagement	Dialogue	Relevancy of knowledge	Discovery
ORGANIZING LEARNING ACTIVITIES	Making the most of options given	Negotiate options	Understand roles and responsibilities of collaborators	Plan learning projects	Understand the non-rational
CRITICAL SKILLS OF EVALUATION	Effective use of evaluation received	Negotiate evaluation processes and standards	Develop evaluation standards and processes	Develop evaluation standards and processes	Reflect against personal experience
THINKING	Selecting best mode	Divergent-creative			Intuitive
SELF-ASSESSMENT AND NEEDS ASSESSMENT		Sense of direction Persistence Realistic goal setting Develop internal structure and control Self-management			

MARK CHEREN: We began putting the competencies into the five domains. We started with cognitive skills. For the nature of knowledge dimension, we said that in the "formal" domain "critical acceptance" describes what the active, conscious learner would be attempting to achieve. We were trying to picture what happens when the desired state is there. In each case we were trying to describe how the ideal post-revolution learner in a domain would operate—not necessarily the way it is now.

MALCOLM KNOWLES: That's critical acceptance of knowledge as defined by somebody else?

MARK CHEREN: Right. Then we put "critical engagement with knowledge" in the open academic situation. In the social, "dialogue" represents the nature of the engagement with knowledge. And then in the personal, there's making personal relevance of knowledge. The "alternate" [or transcendental], is seen as a sort of discovery mode or way of relating to knowledge. Then we included standards in terms of knowledge and found them to be mostly external toward the formal side of the five domains and increasingly internal as one moves across the model. That didn't happen with everything, but it happened with standards.

Turning to "Organizing Learning Activities," there is focus on the cognitive aspect—organizing self to be able to do learning activities in your mind. In the formal we said that making the most of options given is the active conscious role for the learner to play. In the open situation we said that one negotiates options; the initiative can come from all sides, but it's a negotiated affair. Then in the social category, we said that the organizing of the learning activities involves an understanding of effective collaboration. We put under that the roles and responsibilities of the collaborators. The point here is knowing that you're going to organize the learning experience together and knowing how to pull that off; that's the cognitive part of it. There is an interpersonal aspect to negotiating, but you also need the mental map.

Then the personal domain calls for being able to plan learning projects. We were a little uncomfortable as to whether that is equivalent to everything else; but we finally decided to put it down. Planning learning projects is basically what one has to do to organize learning in this category. And finally, alternative or transcendental requires an understanding of the non-rational side of learning. The cognitive part of that is possessing an understanding of it so you can "open that leaf." Also there is needed a little understanding of how you would get yourself ready to learn in this way.

Going across the row called "critical skills of evaluation" we decided that the formal domain requires making good use of the evaluative information given you. The open domain requires negotiating evaluation processes and standards. Involved are negotiations of both the process (how you would be evaluated) and the standards to be used. In the "social" it's important to develop evaluation standards and processes together—that's what is implied. In the "personal" one needs to be able to develop standards and processes for oneself. And in "alternative," since it is essentially non-rational while in progress, competency comes out in subsequent reflection. As Virginia Griffin describes in the article we received for pre-conference reading— thinking about application and reflecting on the experience.

The next category is "thinking." We had a few types of thinking but agreed that basically thinking is pretty much the same across the domains. It involves selecting and applying the appropriate mode of thinking in each domain. The choices are between convergent, divergent, critical, and intuitive. Selecting and applying means choosing from the menu of options and using the right skills for the task at hand. In the formal dimension, critical thinking is paramount and some of us would say there's a lot of convergent thinking required as well. The open context requires a lot of divergent (creative) thinking and also a fair amount of the convergent. We saw considerable similarity in the social domain. In the transpersonal, we were agreed that intuitive thinking is the key.

Then, we tried to see how far we could go with a few of the personal and inter-personal categories of competence (Competency areas II and III). We took the open domain and said, in terms of self-assessment [i.e. Competency II B], what would be going on in the open domain? The individual needs to be able to have a sufficient sense of direction and recognize the relationship between current states and desired goals. The ability to tap in [get credit for?] what's valued in prior learning is also needed, as are self-management skills. Self-management includes maintaining focus—especially important in the open context. Also important under self-management in the open domain are persistence and realistic goal setting. And there's the need to be able to operate with moderate levels of external control and develop internal structure, to be able to non-defensively obtain feedback, seek important feedback, analyze it, make good use of it.

There's one other thing I'd like to say. I believe it's very important to keep in mind (and this is the most important understanding I carry away from the conference) that as we approach learning-how-to-learn and talk about competencies, we are not creating [or dealing with] a separate kind of learning. We shouldn't see ourselves as creating a parallel structure. What's central is how we want to help all learners to become active and conscious learners. To me we're about influencing all learning contexts and domains of knowledge by making the nature of learning in those contexts more active and more conscious.

DAI HOUNSELL: To contrast the approaches used in the two groups [as they went about identifying information to place in various cells of the model], your group's product is perhaps more idealized than ours. I think our focus was something more like specifying good practice (partly) in conventional terms; that is, it isn't necessarily something that is far from what goes on already if we're talking about the formal setting. I think one of the problems is that there isn't a kind of parallelism in (to use Brutus' phrase) "going beyond the information given"—if you like, going beyond the competencies given. As I was listening, I found my mind wandering because the ideas were so good; so the glazed eyes weren't negative reactions. Your distinction between "critical acceptance" and "critical engagement" was wonderful. You get this notion of adherence to norms, but at the same time it's not a passive protest; it's a very very critical distinction. And then distinguishing by using "engagement" along the side seemed superb. Equally fine was your group's notion of making the most of options given—that even in the most apparently passive situations there is scope for control or initiative, and that in any situation, no matter how repressive, you can always find room to breathe.

ALAN KNOX: The way in which our group dealt with those is a little bit like the efforts in role theory. It's like saying, if we're going to develop a paradigm and a theoretical framework, we have to establish some arrays, some variables that are important in role theory and then partition those arrays in such a way that you have some sense of what's low and middle and high. In a sense what we are trying to do is to establish the top end of those arrays. Most of us from experience can talk with reference to a particular cell about what happens when people are at the lowest level of having learned how to learn. But if we could anchor the more ideal end, then we could begin partitioning those arrays, which for analytic and data collection purposes takes you an enormous step further in terms of differentiating among people—in terms of people who are low, in the middle and high in that regard. Also one can then differentiate for a single individual over time and developmentally. That represents progress as a way of conceptualizing having learned how to learn well in a domain.

MALCOLM KNOWLES: There's another dimension that occurs to me. This seems to assume that the entity that's changeable in the picture of learning-how-to-learn is the learner. It occurs to me that the institutions are also changeable and we've found ourselves almost caricaturing (for example) formal institutions—seeing the negative things about them.

DAI HOUNSELL: The open domain was being used partly as a realm for the academic who is actaully creating new knowledge. So if you like, there's a kind of traffic between open and formal all the time in that sort of dimension.

One large issue that I think we did find problematic is exactly what our focus was. We veered between a learning-how-to-learn focus, which tends to become very prescriptive, and a learning focus in terms of what seems to go on at present, which is much more descriptive. And I think in the end what our group's product represents is one in which the focus is learning but from a learning-how-to-learn perspective.

ALAN KNOX: Any other comments or questions about this report from the second group?

RAVINDRA DAVE: In terms of institutional learning vis-a-vis other things that we have mentioned, I think we have to recognize the fact that there is a lot of institutional learning going on around the world. Whether we like it or not, whether it is restrictive or prescriptive, this is the reality. And our thinking has to consider the process of what, for want of a better word, I would call deformalization of formal institutions.

DAI HOUNSELL: But there's another side there too, I think. In some ways it's not so much that we need to sort of pull away from the formal direction as we need to recognize the importance of what goes on in the other domains—to get a more balanced picture of the whole issue of learning; in a sense it's probably possible to find dysfunction in all five of these realms.

RAVINDRA DAVE: That's why I try to keep in view the total life span of an individual. There are certain points in time where the institutionalized learning is more or less prescribed by society. Now, how can we try to create situations which produce optimum possibilities? In school we need to foster competencies or proficiencies for profit from later experiences when it's not necessary to have institutionalized education. And how can we construct the total continuum and not just dichotomize?

DAI HOUNSELL: One way of redressing the balance is to value more what goes on outside the formal setting—to make people feel less modest and reticent about what they've learned outside formal settings. Both the institution and the individual need to value that more.

ALAN KNOX: If time allowed, it would be interesting to start with the personal or social learning and explore how some of the best of formal institutional and open learning could be appropriated or used by both the individual and the group, used in such a way that it still fits and doesn't undermine the modes we've labelled personal and social.

MALCOLM KNOWLES: And vice-versa.

ALAN KNOX: Yes.

MARK CHEREN: As an example of what you're saying, there's the Society for Accelerated Learning, which is meeting in April. They're essentially trying to teach people to take from the alternative or transcendental what can be used to engineer the rest of their learning so as to get more out of it—to take in more information in more efficient ways.

RAVINDRA DAVE: Several studies of developing countries have shown that even when society had not developed far in western terms a lot of cultural and social learning is occurring in the homes and the community, and that the learning is very valuable. Now, when institutions are introduced (for example primary schools), then the academic type of learning begins to enter the society and the local community. Those in charge of institutions also begin to introduce some cultural and social learning. And the findings are that the institutional framework is not strong enough or capable enough perhaps to provide the kind of social and cultural learning that previously was provided by home and local community. Now the question is, how can education be viewed in a more holistic manner, in a more totalistic manner, with certain responsibilities shared by home, community, and school?

THE ROLE
OF
SCHOOLS AND COLLEGES

This matter arose very frequently during the four days of conversations. Several principals identified it as a central interest for them when agenda concerns were first confronted. It surfaced in connection with the question of what learning-how-to-learn "is"—the domain itself. It entered into discussions about competencies and what competencies for lifelong learning should have been developed by the end of secondary school. In conversations about learning to learn in the workplace, it was suggested that persons advocating emphasis on learning to learn in elementary and secondary education might stress with school boards and other educational policy makers the utility of developing learning skills for post-school utilization in the workplace.

In this section the key ideas expressed include the following:

1. Learning-how-to-learn should receive much more attention by administrators, curriculum developers, and instructors in schools and colleges.
2. Tested methods of implementing the learning-how-to-learn idea in schools and colleges are available.
3. It is feasible to deliberately foster motivation and confidence in school children and youth.
4. Learning-how-to-learn has considerable relevance to literacy and adult basic education.
5. Barriers to implementing the learning-how-to-learn concept and process in schools include low level cognitive demands in teaching and evaluation; inertia; inadequate appreciation of the potential

of new technologies and of the implications of a world saturated with information.

6. Insufficient pre-service and in-service education related to the above.

Shortly before the conference adjourned a rather impromptu and informal public symposium was held with the topic "Tomorrow's Schools: Ideal Environments for Learning-How-to-Learn?" Short presentations were made by Patricia Cross, Maurice Gibbons, and Alan Knox, followed by questions and comments from the audience. Jean Moon served as moderator. In addition to the principals, the hundred-odd persons present were largely Northern Illinois University graduate students and faculty members.

JEAN MOON: Tonight our symposium is on "Tomorrow's Schools: Ideal Environments for Learning-How-to-Learn?" Perhaps the emphasis should be on the question mark, because we don't yet have a clear sense, I think, especially in elementary education, of where we're going to go with the concept of learning-how-to-learn. But one thing that is fostering our inquisitiveness about it, our questioning, and our dialogue is an understanding and an assumption that we have certainly been attending to this week: the fact that no education that we receive will last us for a lifetime. And that's a fact that we have to think about the implications for, and deal with the consequences of. Perhaps what we want to turn our attention to this evening is the possibility of teaching our children the skills and attitudes that will be required of them as lifelong learners. This afternoon, for instance, we tried to break out competencies and proficiencies for lifelong learning.

Personally I have a scholarly interest in this subject; my area of focus is on teachers and how they perceive their own learning. And I look upon their perception in relationship to the framework of learning styles. I also have a personal interest in this subject, having turned my five year old son Doug over to public education this year. Now if I sound nervous about this, I am. As I've evaluated what his education has brought him this past seven or eight months, I find that he now knows how to raise his hand effectively, how to stand in line, how to ride the bus, not to ask for snacks, and not to go to the bathroom too often. I'm sure he's learned other things too. I make the point that schools are about other things besides content and that they have been for a long time. They've been trying to be about creating and implanting the skills for becoming effective citizens. It may mean that we need to look at other process skills that enable people to become effective lifelong learners.

THREE PRESENTATIONS

Patricia Cross is the Chair and Professor of Administration, Planning, and Social Policy at Harvard University. Her interests over the years have included populations that have not been traditionally served by our educational institutions, and the responses by educational institutions to those particular populations. A long-standing interest, as I understand it, is college teaching, looking at ways that it can be improved. We have also with us Maurice Gibbons from Simon Fraser University, Vancouver, who has interests in curriculum development, self-education, education in global issues, and the transformation of schools. And this evening he's going to share some research that he's been doing in several of those areas. And we have Alan Knox from the University of Wisconsin-Madison who is Professor of Continuing Education. His interests include adult education, community education, program evaluation and many other aspects. He has a forthcoming book on helping adults to learn in a variety of settings and making connections between the learning and teaching acts.

PATRICIA CROSS: The question we were asked to address tonight is the following: Tomorrow's Schools, Ideal Environments for Learning-How-to-Learn? As you probably know—at least you should know if you've observed this conference—most academics like to begin by first defining their terms. In the first place, in order to answer that question, we need to know, what is tomorrow? Is tomorrow the schools five years hence, ten years hence, or twenty years hence? Then we need to know how rigorous we're going to be in interpreting the words "ideal environment." And I'm going to suggest that we settle for interpreting ideal environments as: is this in any way possible? Then for my own purposes I'm going to define schools as any kind of institution purporting to teach students, including colleges and universities.

So, now as you can see, I have worked a subtle transformation in the question I was assigned to one that I think I might have some hope of answering. So the new question is this: colleges five or ten years hence: is there any chance that they will be supportive of learning-how-to-learn?

Let me begin by describing college learning environments as they exist today as viewed through the eyes of people doing research on college teaching. If we put all of the studies that have been done on that in the last decade together, we would come out with something very very close to what Joe Axelrod described as the four teaching prototypes for college students.

First we have Professor A whose goal is to cover the subject matter in a rather systematic and orderly fashion, presenting the facts and principles and then testing students on their comprehension and their understanding of those principles and facts of the discipline. He regards knowledge as a product rather than a process; his style of teaching is ordinarily to use lectures, but occasionally he uses discussions, primarily to determine whether the students comprehend the material. He works very hard on "covering" the subject matter in his class, and his evaluation approach usually consists of short answer tests to which he assigns numerical scores because most questions can be graded as right answers.

Then we have Professor B. He is one of the most colorful figures on campus, and his goal in teaching is to demonstrate how the educated mind works. His style is to lecture, and his purpose is to provide a model for students, to give students a demonstration of how a person who is really competent in a discipline attacks that discipline. He makes no attempt to cover the subject matter because he regards learning as process rather than product. His evaluation tends to be asking the students to demonstrate that they are educated persons in the use of their minds. Now, Professors A and B both represent teacher-centered styles. So that in Professor A you have teacher as the authority and in Professor B you have teacher as model. You could put mottos with those, and Professor A's would be, "I teach what I know;" and Professor B's would be, "I teach what I am."

Now the next two styles are student-centered. Professor C: The goal is to promote the cognitive development of students. Professor C would ordinarily concentrate on the higher levels of the Bloom taxonomy of cognitive skills, focussing more on asking students to analyze, to synthesize, and to evaluate rather than simply to recall and recognize and comprehend. He would ordinarily in teaching style use a discussion method or Socratic method or perhaps the case study, primarily to see how people are developing in terms of cognition. The evaluation would ordinarily consist of essay exams or problem solving stressing analysis. The motto for Professor C would then be: I develop minds.

And then the last prototype I will call Professor D. Like C he is student centered and his goal is to develop the whole person. Professor D would ordinarily be very informal in teaching style, would quite frequently serve as facilitator of the learning group, would have a lot of off-campus and on-campus interactions with students, would know all students by name, and would ordinarily know a good deal of their backgrounds and their current concerns. He would steer clear pretty much of hard-nosed evaluation and instead would diagnose for learning development. His motto would be: I develop people.

Now, of these four prototypes which are fairly consistent throughout the research, far and away the most common is Professor A—the teaching of facts and principles of the covering of subject matter. And that is fairly closely followed by Professor C—the "I develop minds emphasis on cognitive growth." Professors B and D are relatively rare in college faculties.

In those first few minutes I've tried to lay out a revised question; I've tried to describe what the current situation is; and like all academics, I am trying to avoid answering directly any question to which there is no answer. So what I am going to do, instead, is to propose an answer to this question by asking you four questions: first, virtually all college teachers receive their professsional training in the disciplinary departments of graduate schools. Question: What chance is there that graduate faculties will require knowledge of teaching and learning within the next ten years?

Second, present educational reform movements are moving strongly in the direction of mandated statewide testing—short answers, easily scorable. Historically, educational reform movements have consisted of fairly wild swings of the pendulum from what society regards as too permissive to what society eventually comes to regard as too rigid, and back again. Question: How long will it take for us to conclude that we have gone too far (with information doubling every five and a half years) in the teaching of easily measured facts and that that is counterproductive?

Third, the demographic situation today is that college students are quite scarce but college faculty are quite plentiful. So institutions with really rather mediocre academic reputations these days are quite pleased to discover that they are able to attract prospective faculty members from highly research-oriented universities, many of them with an established research reputation. Researchers point to a "research surge" that is now taking place in institutions that used to be primarily teaching institutions. By that they mean that in considering faculty members for promotion, there's more emphasis on research and publications—particularly number of publications. Question: How long will it take to turn the criteria for academic excellence from the reputation of the faculty to the quality of student learning taking place on that campus?

Finally, with scientific and technical information now doubling every five and a half years (or so we are told) and with students forgetting the information that their teachers work so hard to tell them, I assume that traditional education is now on a collision course with the information society. A [fourth] question for you, then, is as follows: How long will it take for us to conclude that learning-how-to-learn is the only education worth pursuing for students, for educators, and for society?

MAURICE GIBBONS: I wish to thank all of you here who are at all responsible for this wonderful opportunity to talk with so many esteemed colleagues and have the absolute luxury of being able to sit down for several days and discuss those issues that are of greatest concern to us in such a hospitable environment. It is truly wonderful and I am deeply appreciative of this opportunity; it has just been glorious.

I think that we are faced with a crisis in education; I think it's a benevolent crisis; and anything that starts to gather and gives us pressure to move is also an opportunity. I believe the Chinese character for danger also means opportunity.

In thinking about this, I was really impressed that in the last five decades there's been more momentous change in any individual decade than in any century we can think of. I think for instance of the forties and the introduction of the nuclear age. I think of the fifties and the introduction of the television age which brought the world into every home almost wherever it is. I think of the sixties which brought in the space age which gave us the first opportunity to look at our world from out in space. I think of the seventies as essentially a computer age information and computers—and the incredible transformation of our ability and the extension of our nervous systems that that permits. And what is it going to be in this decade? Kinetic engineering, artificial intelligence, lasers, space travel, space colonization - who knows what it's going to be, because even from last night to tonight, the rate at which information doubles has gone from eight years to five and a half. [laughter]

For these reasons I think learning-how-to-learn is just an incredibly important topic.

The most important thing I think that I can do is tell you what I am doing. It isn't exactly research, although some research has been involved and some publications about research; mostly it's been an attempt to solve problems in the schools, working with schools, experiment with new programs, and so on. And so my work has been mostly field-based, and I would like to talk to you about some of those conceptual programs which we've worked with in the schools.

Just to lay a bit of groundwork. Learning-how-to-learn involves both learning-how-to-learn in school and for learning afterward as well. So it's really a split in that direction as well. It seems to me that we are concerned first of all with teaching students how to learn in their subjects, in their classes; we're also trying to teach them, implicit in this slogan, for lifelong learning as well. So the student has to know not only what to learn, what the teacher tells him within the school, the student also has to be taught how to learn it. I think some of the research demonstrates very clearly that very often students are simply told to learn, they are not taught how to learn. They are given the information, given the assignment, but seldom taught the strategies by which to learn what has been assigned to them.

So, there's teaching students the content and the strategies that they need at the same time so that they can master that content. The second part of that is to teach in such a way that they learn how to decide, how to choose, how to set goals, how to plan, how to, in other words, manage the whole curriculum for themselves. Because that indeed is one of the ways of formulating what lifelong learning is—the ability to design productive programs for yourself and with others for the rest of your life, and to be an active learner. I think it's a really worthwhile goal. Somehow we have to communicate to people that learning is just the most exciting way to be in the world if we consider it openly. Learning, working with others on good projects, making a difference and being productive is just the highest form I think of "being" that one can aspire to and the most exciting.

With these tasks before us there are strong implications for programs and I'd like to describe to you some of the programs. One of the things that distinguishes them is that it not only means teaching content, it not only means teaching processes and strategies, it also means somehow impacting the inner states, the attitudes, the visions, the enthusiasm, the emotion of students as well.

So that is a third dimension, if you like: besides the content, besides the structure and process and skills, to somehow find a way to create the drive and initiative. Some of the capacities that we've been working with specifically have been clarity—you can't set a goal unless you have an inner sense of clarity about yourself. You can't take initiative unless you have drive. You can't really lay a plan unless you have the confidence that it can be achieved. Others that we're concerned with are determination, openness to evaluative feedback, and also reflection on distancing and reflecting on the experience that you have. And if any of you are interested, we have worked on some instrumentation to encourage students to do that.

The programs I've developed (and developed with others) include, first of all a "walkabout program." The walkabout program is essentially a response to many schools' failure to pay attention to the transition that children face when they graduate and have to go out and become adults—an incredible psychosocial transition and vocational transition and relational transition as well. What we did first—over a decade ago—was to set up programs, design programs, field test them. Some are still in operation; for other schools the program has become a kind of approach that is absorbed and modified for their own uses (Gibbons and Phillips, 1982).

The student is taught the process of planning and then is taught the process of challenging self to reach as far as he or she believes is feasible in these six areas: academic concentration, logical inquiry, creative expression, practical application, service, and adventure. Part of that sense of building emotion is the focus on demonstration at the end— the public demonstration where students actually demonstrate what they set out to do and what they achieved, what they are now able to do that they couldn't when they started. It becomes a kind of enrichment of the whole idea of what a goal really is. The celebration honors the risk that was taken by the student, the achievement they made, and helps to set the platform for the next activity. This can be done as a special program. It's been operated in school and out; it can be a special program, two weeks devoted to it or a month or spread out during the year. It can be a course or a whole program.

The other thing we've attempted to do is to expand that into a challenge program. It simply says what would it be like if students were asked to pursue excellence—let's say to be able by the end of grade twelve to take the last semester's work and be completely responsible for its design and implementation.

The question is, what would the previous eleven and a half years be like in order to prepare them to do that with excellence?

We've worked on a number of others. One is the Experts Program. It says that most of our courses are "coverage" courses—survey courses, that cover broad bodies of information. The Expert's Program says: all right there has to be a time when students are encouraged to select a field and go in deep. We encourage that to begin very early on— even in kindergarten. We've had a couple of school systems which have started that. We think that should be a part of the process right through school.

These are just a few of the things that we are trying to do to implement the whole idea of learning-how-to-learn in schools and classrooms and with adults.

ALAN KNOX: As I consider learning-how-to-learn in schools and colleges, as with many other matters it seems to me I can look at it like a glass—it's either half empty or half full. And as I think about learning-how-to-learn in such settings and take the sort of pessimistic stand, I am concerned with the keen competition that exists for the talent that might enter teacher training programs. There is now such a wide range of career options available to both men and women (who were widely available as school teachers formerly) that I become distressed in terms of the schools' being able not only to cover the necessary content and also to take responsibility in the area of learning-how-to-learn. As I think of higher education and the priorities that exist in some institutions (in terms of research versus teaching) and consider the way in which schools and colleges seem to be organized, it seems to me that they are not organized to make sure that learners really understand the content, let alone to insure that they learn how to learn. It's almost as though colleges were largely social mechanisms for sorting people by providing a kind of a gross test of intelligence and motivation.

When I look at the part of the glass of water that is half full, however, it seems to me that there is increasingly widespread recognition throughout our society of the essentiality of lifelong learning. And this has an impact on how parents and teachers and administrators and other people connected with schools and colleges are viewing education. They are increasingly coming to understand that education is broadly diffused throughout the society, that schools and colleges are only part of the picture, and that perhaps provides pressure to look more broadly at education's role. And I see available some aspects of technology that put more control in the hands of the individual learner, so that he has a free hand to deal with learning and is not restricted to what he can get from a lecture or a course. One can go beyond classrooms to videotapes, to computer simulation, and other technological sources of access to information and ideas.

In that more optimistic vein, I'll explore two examples for a few minutes—one aimed mainly at elementary-secondary schools and the other at higher education.

The schools' example grows out of the current concern for the short supply of school teachers—particularly in secondary schools and especially in such fields as math and science. There are insufficient numbers of people being trained as secondary school science teachers who know very much about science. And the number of people already teaching and teaching well seems to be very restricted; I think that's a crisis area in secondary education right now. An alternative is employing large numbers of people to teach high school science who do not know very much about science.

It seems to me that there is one alternative to do something about this problem that's not likely to change very much, given the very attractive opportunities outside of teaching for people with science preparation. That is to borrow from the community education concept and bring school children out into the community and bring the community into the schools. In almost every community there are people with a high degree of preparation, with background in various scientific fields who could make an enormous contribution to high school students.

A way of trying to sidestep some of the expected resistance to that notion (of using non-certified teachers) would be (on an interim basis) to arrange for engineers and scientists as resource persons for the instructional program—and by necessity to involve students in learning how to learn from such resources. This knowledge should serve them well as high school students and for the rest of their lives in dealing with scientific content.

My other example is at the higher education level in an aspect of medical science. It concerns something that's going on in a relatively few places in North America, and one is at Southern Illinois University's medical school in Springfield. People like Howard Barrows and Robin Tamblyn in their book on problem-based learning [Problem-based Learning, Springer, 1980] describe very well the following procedure. And that is to train, very carefully, people to be simulated patients, to be so good at it that a practicing physician has a difficult time knowing who is a simulated patient and who is a real patient, even in terms of symptoms one picks up with a stethescope. Those simulated patients are examined by medical students who request computer generated lab tests that go along with the simulated patient and go through a videotaped interview and examination process with that simulated patient. After doing that, the students are provided with some expert feedback regarding their diagnosis, and they also receive feedback from the simulated patient's standpoint, which many times medical students and physicians do not receive. Then the student views a videotape of that simulated patient going through the diagnostic workup by an expert diagnostician in order to provide a standard of excellence against which to compare the clinical process the medical student went through. Then the two are compared and the student can return to the videotape to view himself against what was done by the expert diagnostician dealing with the same symptoms and the same patient. He or she then sits down with other medical students, faculty members, and others to review those differences and receives a computer-generated output having to do with the similarities and differences between student and expert diagnoses and recommended plan of action, and is able to see clearly the discrepancy between his or her behavior and a standard of best practice. Then after discussion and further targeted reading on topics that deal with discrepancies between performance and recommended or achievable best practice, the student can repeat the activity with another simulated patient or another problem area.

So you have practice, you have standards, you have feedback and a chance to try it again and again. Beautifully illuminated, it seems to me in Barrows and Tamblyn is a whole host of arrangements for feedback and guidance, not only about the content of medicine but about the learning process and the effectiveness of the process that the physician-to-be uses to understand that content, to understand learning strategies, and to understand how they relate to clinical practice. It seems to me that those two examples suggest some very specific ways in which we could be optimistic about schools and colleges helping people learn-how-to-learn.

BARRIERS TO LEARNING-HOW-TO-LEARN

Participant: I'd be interested in what the panel members believe to be critical barriers in schooling and in school to learning-how-to-learn.

Patricia Cross: One of the barriers that disturbs me a great deal at the moment is the present direction of the school reform movement—the movement's directions seem to be toward students' learning how to give quick, easy answers on answer sheets that are easily scoreable. And that of course is a legislative problem and it's interpreted as standards, but it seems to me it's incorrectly interpreted that way. What we're using as standards now is how much is learned rather than what is learned and how it's learned. So that's one barrier.

The other barrier I didn't mention that bothers me a good deal in higher education is some research that was done recently in an Arizona community college in which the researcher discovered that the predominant mode of teaching in that college was what he called "bitting." Bitting is when you provide isolted bits of information with no overall framework. He discovered that to be the way the teachers responded to the perceived low ability of their students who (as in community colleges nationwide) had eighth grade reading levels. Teachers were teaching down, making very low level cognitive demands, by presenting bits of information. Students were responding by trying their best to recall and recognize those bits of information. With the result that we were going again in exactly the opposite direction to learning-how-to-learn. Those are two examples of impediments to what we're talking about at this conference.

ALAN KNOX: If we contrast educational programs for children with those for adults we find usually a more active learner role and concern for meaning and understanding on the part of the participants in adult education than in preparatory education. And a non-barrier, if you will, for adults is the fact that they usually are there voluntarily and can "vote with their feet," having lots of other alternatives for learning what they want to learn.

By contrast, it seems to me a very high percentage of young people in elementary, secondary, and higher education do not see themselves as volunteers for learning. They see it as some sort of mandatory arrangement. Now once you have that mind set on the part of the learners, it is very difficult for teachers to avoid getting into a sort of a rut, of taking the whole thing for granted. Because within, in some relatively broad range, the students are still going to be there, the curriculum is still going to be there, your job is still going to be there.

If learning-how-to-learn includes learners' having a very active role, possessing a sense of the problem before information is presented to them, involving them in some of the decisions about what's going to be covered and evaluated and so on, then I see the lack of that voluntariness as being a barrier.

MAURICE GIBBONS: I have a concern, a very practical one and one that concerns us all, because I believe that practitioners, certainly the people in the field that I work with, are as concerned about change as people who sit like me in their offices in the university and dream about possible paradigms.

We can see a future coming. I see everybody soon using a very small computer, being hooked up to the entire world—which you can do right now. It's not the future; this is now. One can hook up to virtually anywhere in the world, talk with people, confer with them, exchange information, tap into incredible databases, hook up with programs, communicate with groups of people like the one that's been meeting here, access information, carry files, and so on.

The future isn't tomorrow, or five years hence—the future is now. And it's coming at an incredible rate. I understand that AT&T is developing a million megabite chip. An encyclopedia could be in one small corner of this little thing that would fit in your watch and it would be readily accessible to you. It's incredible—even a fraction of that.

So as the future hurtles upon us, and I think that maybe we are hermetically sealed, whether we're at the college or in the school, we're hermetically sealed from the influences that cause change. The very small, carry-around computer (which I take to be as the arrow was to knighthood, the canon was to the castle, etc.) maybe should be welcomed. Maybe the technology will liberate us to teach people processes, to encourage them to grow and deal with the issues of learning-how-to-learn. Because some of the things which the computer does, and does extremely well and is getting better at all the time, can take some of those more mechanical kinds of aspects of teaching off our hands.

So I think of it as high teach as well as high tech. They go together—high teach, high touch, and high tech.

Also, the hierarchical nature of our decision making pattern locks us in. The future that we can start to see is affected by the way learning is hooked in with management. Most of the decisions in schools seem to be management decisions that don't have a lot to do with preferred approaches to learning. It's a good system for managing, sorting, managing, grading, and moving people on. It's not really designed for learning and learning-how-to-learn.

One of the things I think that we lack is a sense of the next paradigm. Do we agree we are quite clearly on the verge of a paradigm shift? There's just no foreseeable way of coping with the future going on the way we are. Or even coping with the present, hardly. So the thing is that we are, if you agree with me, on the edge of a paradigm shift which will change everything. Either with us or without us. And the thing that we lack, perhaps, is a way to start to crack this hermetically sealed system which we seem helpless to do very much about—except by putting people out in alternative settings or by making cosmetic changes within. Perhaps the start needs to begin with achieving a shared vision—a shared vision of how we want schools to be and how they will have to be to meet the future that we see coming. We cannot deal with the present; we have to start to anticipate the future and start to deal with that. And that's true of all the crises we face globally.

So one of the things that I think that we might do to break this fixed paradigm which we don't seem to be able to get out of is perhaps to start to build a shared vision. And maybe one of the elements in that shared vision—a powerful one because we can start to work on it tomorrow without anyone's approval—is a vision of learning-how-to-learn.

FACULTY DEVELOPMENT

PARTICIPANT: I'd like to address this mainly to Professor Cross. I'm wondering about the implications for staff development of part-time teachers of adults—of helping them employ the learning-how-to-learn idea, or helping their students to learn how to learn when they themselves may never have learned how to teach let alone learn. Many of the part-timers that I'm talking about are people who come out of skill areas, content areas, let's say accountants who teach an accounting course in a community college.

PATRICIA CROSS: I think you may have a point in that some of the part-time teachers may not have very good learning skills themselves. On the other hand I would maintain that perhaps somebody teaching auto mechanics in a kind of hands-on problem solving way is closer to what we're talking about in learning-how-to-learn than the full-time history teacher who stands up and conducts the history lesson as teaching-as-telling and hopes that something will remain in student minds about history. So I wouldn't accept without a good deal of thought the notion that part-time teachers are necessarily at a disadvantage.

Now, having said that, I would go along to say I think one of our greatest problems in community colleges and university teaching is simply the question of in-service training. That is for part-time teachers, for full-time teachers, for two-year colleges, for my own institution—a research university primarily—there is nothing done to break the cycle of teaching-as-telling.

Students as they go through grad school are not exposed to learning-how-to-learn concepts or relevant styles of teaching. And so there is nothing that would give them any different notion that there are other ways to teach. So part of the obligation of adult educators ought to be the in-service training of both full and part-time teachers.

LITERACY AND BASIC EDUCATION

Participant: Wanda Cook [Adult Literacy in the United States, International Association, 1977] states that there will always be a certain amount of illiteracy because there are some people who just don't want to learn and therefore cannot be reached. First of all, do you agree with this? And secondly, how does the concept of learning-how-to-learn impact this group?

Alan Knox: There may well be within the total adult population some relatively, a small residual group of people who have very great difficulty learning. But that proportion of the total adult population is so small, it seems to me, that it hardly provides any excuse for explaining away perhaps a quarter to a third of the adult population who are functionally illiterate in this country.

I do believe that learning-how-to-learn is a very relevant concept for them, but it requires a broadening of that concept. And that is not seeing learning-how-to-learn as equivalent to learning how to read, or study skills—or learning to survive in school systems. What is needed is looking far more broadly at learning-how-to-learn in many settings, not just in educational institutions but in the family, in the neighborhood, and in the workplace and in the church and in the community organizations and the like, and to take into account the particular life styles of people who are involved.

With adults who have the lowest levels of formal education, you find that there is relatively little use of print media, technology, and experts for information serving purposes. For organized learning the main dependence is on oral communication. It's conversation, talking with people one knows and trusts—for making health decisions, legal decisions, job seeking decisions and so on. And so it seems to me if you're concerned about that population and learning-how-to-learn, a starting point is to appreciate first the very high level of learning that some people have attained—in terms of listening and remembering, for example. They develop strategies: asking people to repeat, asking the same question to two or three people until you've got it (because you can't write it down), for example. They can't access the print media and other ways of learning. So begin by recognizing their successful experiences and strengths and help them to build upon those—rather than coming with a deficiency model that says you are inadequate because you don't know how to read.

Secondly, help them to broaden their learning repertoires by starting with the sorts of issues that grab them, where they do know the problem, where they do know the question and are prepared to seek answers and seek solutions because they're already engaged—along the lines of the Freire approach.

So it seems to me that not only is learning-how-to-learn relevant for those low in literacy, it seems to me that unless we're to have a two class system with a vengeance, it is essential that we do something about that. And we know some things right now that can help to do it.

RELATIONSHIPS BETWEEN TEACHING, LEARNING, AND LEARNING-HOW-TO-LEARN

In the following excerpts two European scholars treat this topic through brief descriptions of their own experience and research.

In the first section, Dai Hounsell is speaking; in the second, Roger Säljö.

For indepth exploration of this area, the reader can turn to Marton, Hounsell, and Entwistle's *The Experience of Learning* and Graham Gibb's *Teaching Students to Learn*.

DAI HOUNSELL: I'm going to try to quickly give something of the flavor of what's been called the European contributions to learning and learning-how-to-learn. I suppose one of the most obvious starting points is that our concern has been with the difference, a major one, between how faculty and students view and understand the learning/teaching process. And I can best capture that in a statement by an Australian: "Learning at a university is like trying to drink water from a fire hydrant."

So that's really the first point I want to make, that our concern really has been not to take the phenomenon of learning for granted. In other words to assume that we already know what learning is and what it means to students and therefore we can design learning to learn experiences accordingly. But instead, to see learning as something that we don't yet fully understand, something that is yet to be disclosed. And that's meant, in terms of the research, trying to describe and to understand learning as it's experienced by learners themselves.

113

From this investigation what we arrive at are qualitative differences in how and what students learn. And I can't do justice to the many qualitative differences that have emerged, so what I'm going to do very self-interestedly is to simply give you one example from some recent work of my own and try and put that into some sort of wider context. What I'm going to very briefly look at is a kind of summary of the findings from a study of essay-writing by undergraduates. Now I understand that in America you have things like term papers and assignments and so on; I think for many British students, particularly in the arts and social sciences and the humanities generally, essay-writing seems like what university is about because that's what they spend most of their time doing. Between eighteen and twenty three-thousand word essays in a year is not at all an unusual demand.

Broadly speaking, what do we find when we look at essay-writing as an activity for undergraduates in a subject like history? My essential finding was that students had differences in their conceptions of what essay-writing meant and of what essay-writing involved in history as a discipline. And I'll just briefly try and make the distinction between these two conceptions. The first one, which is obviously qualitatively more sophisticated and clearly also what the faculty members are expecting is a notion of argument and ordered presentation of a distinctive point of view substantiated by evidence. In other words, if you like, we've actually got three interrelated elements making up that conception. On the one hand, there's a distinctive point of view expected of the student, which we often talk about as the argument itself—what you've got to say. And there is a second element which has to do with order and logic and coherence. And a third element which has to do with evidence and substantiation.

What we find among the same group of students,

studying history as their major subject and at a fairly advanced stage in their studies, is a quite different conception of what essay-writing in history is about. They see history writing as an ordered presentation of facts and ideas. In other words, that first element that I talked about, the interpretive one—of the notion that you are presenting a distinctive point of view—is not present. And the notion is simply that you can enrich your essay by putting in a few ideas and thoughts of your own. Similarly, there is a concern with order and with logicality, but not with the ordered presentation of that distinctive viewpoint. And then, evidence, the whole issue of data, if you like, is seen much more in terms of quantitative accumulation of facts which you pile in to the essay itself.

Without going into much greater detail, these results mirror a much more basic distinction which we found in a lot of work from student learners and that's very broadly a distinction between learning as a kind of quest for meaning and understanding as opposed to learning as a kind of reproductive activity concerned with regurgitation—giving back material to the teacher—in a fairly unthinking way. Let me try to look briefly at the sort of implications of this. It seems to me firstly that it has implications for what, at least in Europe, we would regard as the traditional approach to learning-how-to-learn, which tends to get labelled as study skills—the inculcation of general purpose study techniques. The first implication of the kind of research that we're talking about is that study skills in vacua, if you like, isolated from a disciplinary context—isolated from a course setting—can't actually make much headway. But if we give students training in things like organizing their time, essay planning, style, punctuation and so on, all of those things won't make much of a difference in terms of the kind of conceptions that we're talking about. But instead we might see the focal issue in cases like this as bound up with something that I want to call, perhaps rather grandly "the nature of academic discourse." This refers to the "grammar of study" with a discipline—the norms, the principles, the rules by which academics, specialists within a particular discipline, communicate with one another. It also involves what they understand to be the nature of their discipline and its way of looking at the world as a form of inquiry.

Equally fundamentally, it seems to me that if we take that as the focal issue we're concerned with an obvious teaching problem—how do we wean students away from that reproductive conception to one that's much more concerned with meaning. I think the most important point to be made is that we cannot see that issue as merely information giving, with, if you like, simply giving students information or guidelines about our own expectations. The gulf between their understanding of what's involved and what's expected and our understanding, the gulf between the premises and underlying assumptions, is far too large for that. And so, I think what we're really concerned with—whether we think of this as a basic teaching problem or as a learning-how-to-learn problem—is something like a shared understanding of academic expectations and certainly within the European context, that's a long way from most people's understanding of what study skills or learning-how-to-learn mean.

ROGER SALJO: My interest in the area of learning and learning-how-to-learn starts from an observation that has been made by many who have read introductory textbooks on learning. Namely that the authors very early on regret that they can't give a satisfactory definition of what it means to learn. They try to do so and definitions become long and empty because of the sort of generalized language which they have to use in order to cover all possible aspects of learning.

To me this is a very interesting starting point for

analyzing learning because the consequence of this could be that there is nothing common to all the elements that we refer to as learning—that are really quite disparate matters. I became interested in this phenomenon. Instead of trying to define learning, together with a lot of colleagues, I began asking people what they did when they were at university, how they spent their time, what they were doing, and so forth.

A very interesting example or illustration appeared in these contexts. When we asked people questions like, "Could you give me an example of something really significant that you think you've learned?," they very seldom referred to the formal context of the university. They would always go beyond that and say, "I learned something, you know, which had great personal meaning to me when I had a child or when I was sick." So they were using the term learning with qualifications like real learning, genuine learning to talk about things outside the university.

The problem of learning to me, in still being interested in the psychological aspects, is a problem of how knowledge is reproduced in society, at a very general level. And this reproduction of knowledge is a necessary element of social development. We have to build on what we've got; we have to go further. Even animals do this; they sort of develop skills which are unique to a particular group of animals living in a particular context and they build on these so the next generation can go further. This reproduction of knowledge at a very general sense takes place in either formal or informal settings, and the informal settings are very important. In such context we learn many things that are not formally provided in the educational system. We learn at best how to behave, how to treat other people, how to ride a bicycle, and all sorts of things that are necessary for living in society but which are not necessarily considered objects of teaching in formal settings.

In formal settings, and I restrict myself here to the school, it's obvious that there are lots of activities going on which people tend to classify as teaching and learning. But our experience from the beginning was, if you looked at it and if you followed people around for a day or a week or if you interviewed them about what they were doing, there were significant differences in how they behaved, how they acted.

So learning did not seem to be a commonly experienced activity; it was only common when you talked about it at a very general level. Basically what I became interested in was the kind of learning that was characteristic of schooling, at least in the kinds of educational institutions that I studied. And it was a kind of knowledge, a kind of learning, of transmittence of knowledge which is very typical for a literate culture, a literate society. It was a high reliance on explicit verbal definitions and explicit knowledge (phrased I think by David Alston as "prose statements known to be true"). This is what was taught and learned by students in these settings. There are very strong historical reasons for this. We developed long ago this formal institution of the school with this literate mode of knowing—knowledge is what is in the book. We came to develop very definite notions about what is correct and what is not correct and we developed strong rules about all sorts of formal aspects like spelling and so on. And as soon as schools appeared, by the way, we began to have learning problems and problems of motivation. These problems do not appear in informal contexts to the same extent and are not as frequently encountered in societies that rely less on formal schooling than we do.

In my experience and in the discussions we've had here, I think there are unrealistic assumptions about what schools can do. Schools are basically designed or built up to deal with this kind of explicit, literate type of knowledge. We could wish them to do other things, but that's difficult because they rely on the literate tradition.

Anyway, my general point with relation to the phenomenon of learning is that these students—and people in general, and even the teachers that we observed—seemed to mean very different things by learning. Their world was not homogenous. If you'd ask someone in his first term of graduate studies, he would say one thing, define learning in one way. And if you came back and asked him a few years later, chances are very high that he would have changed, that he would say something else. For example, there was a strong difference between those who defined learning as giving back what's in the book (being passive recipients of knowledge that others had produced) and others who saw themselves as agents of learning or determiners of knowledge (the real producers in this situation). Then we got interested in where these two conceptions come from and why it is that people experience learning in this way. We first thought that these were individual personality differences in people. But it turned out that the only time that most of these people identified learning with these kinds of memorizing activities was when they perceived the situation as a school context; that was the only time that they used these kinds of strategies.

PHILOSOPHICAL CONCERNS

A not inconsiderable portion of the principals' discussion dealt with goals, standards, values, and ethics. Among the questions and issues were the following:

1. Learning-How-to-Learn for What? For Whom?
2. What Value Assumptions are Reflected in the Concept?
3. To What Extent Should Individualism in Learning be Fostered?
4. How is Empowerment Involved?
5. Are There Potential Contributions to Understanding and Peace?

A significant fact here is that these issues were not scheduled to be examined. They emerged through the cut and thrust of dialogue, and communication about them was often accompanied by a high level of intensity and interest.

OF VALUES AND ASSUMPTIONS

MAURICE GIBBONS: How essential is the value consideration in learning-how-to-learn? Because what we've got here is—perhaps we are describing a machine. Where does the energy come from to drive this machine?

RONALD CERVERO: [to another principal] Is that the same thing you're talking about? I think you're saying that this discussion is confusing the descriptive with the prescriptive. Are we saying that if you've learned to learn you're a better person?

ROGER SALJO: No, I was thinking of what has been done here as an attempt to describe how people develop and grow, and I was wondering how essential it was to hold these what for me seem to be certain hidden value assumptions instead of trying to achieve a more neutral language despite our different orientations. I think we can run into problems otherwise.

MARK CHEREN: That seems like a good question to ask in an international context because I've always assumed that the rationale, the moral rationale that we probably do share is that the basis of most morality is ultimately species' survival. And that what we're arguing when we try to promote learning-how-to-learn is something like this: it's no longer good enough for people to accept transmitted learning. You have to learn faster; each of us needs access to information from several different points in order to have the chance of being able to do a job and earn a living, much less survive collectively. And I thought there was a kind of implicit morality in all that—one that says we have to learn how to learn because the old ways of transmitting knowledge that allowed you to play a more passive role weren't globally conducive to the continuation of the species. Is that something we all agree on?

RONALD CERVERO: Well I would say this is a very individualistic viewpoint. There would be collective viewpoints that would see this as a real negative, and if you want to talk values, it seems to me you have to deal with basic issues. You're individuating people more and more this way and if you think that's a positive, ok. It's a value call, and I think you could argue clearly that by individuating you're breaking society apart.

ROBERT SMITH: It might be difficult to offer a workshop in Kiev on developing self-directedness in learning. You'd have to clear it I'm sure—at least that's what we are told about that society. They would not necessarily welcome our working toward making people more self-directed. Am I right?

RAVINDRA DAVE: Well, the point is to think in a context that says what would be a value system in which, while individuals are allowed to grow, their collectivity is not neglected—a dynamic and interactive balance between the two. If self-directed learning were properly explained and understood [in a socialist state], then probably there would be less of an objection. But very often the word "self" creates an image that this is something anti-collective (which of course it is not).

We [UNESCO] have a project in five socialist countries on what is called self-instruction or autonomous instruction. And all the countries are participating in an excellent manner; it's been going on for the last three years. But the thing is that "autonomy" is interpreted in one way in one society and in another way in another society. So they accept autonomous learning. But where one puts a mark on the continuum is an issue. And what is needed is to see the different points of view. Just as individualization versus collectivism in a value system are viewed differently, we have to begin to formulate what might be called range definitions of certain things rather than point definitions. Point definitions have created certain problems which don't permit a wide area of collaboration. And that is where the value matter lies. Certainly there are different value systems which we must accept, but then within this there are certain areas of commonality which also should be recognized.

TOWARD ONE WORLD

RAVINDRA DAVE: There's a good deal of talk about education for peace. We're all aware of the threat of global war. How do we look at this process in the context of achievement of peace? Is there thinking being done about this by those interested in transpersonal learning? I'm not saying that we turn this group into peace education; that's not my idea. But to concretize this thing as much as possible, and on the other hand reflect on some of the common elements, I'd just like to have your reaction to this.

MAURICE GIBBONS: I feel that the natural extension of learning-how-to-learn is a challenge dimension. It's a dynamic reaching-forward kind of dimension that can be part of all learning-how-to-learn programs particularly as they become separate from institutions. And part of that challenge as it reaches outward, as it comes outside the institution, is what kind of person am I going to be? And what kind of responsibilities do I have? I see that as on the expanding pattern which ultimately must be global. In fact, if there is a characteristic of our time, my sense is that it is likely that global considerations are going to be part of a new trend along with technology.

We've identified sort of five central issues that are related to that global setting. One is global citizenship, taking an expanded view of responsibility. Second is membership in the family of mankind, in the sense that we are all members of the same family. Third is stewardship of earth—balancing, management enhancement. The fourth is peaceful or negotiated resolution of conflict. And the fifth is designing the future as distinct from letting the future happen. And what we're starting and trying to develop within schools and within individuals is the idea that it's not going to happen by leaving it to management—in the political and governmental sense. That each of us has a responsibility and a capacity to make a difference. And this introduces the second feature that says that it's not only a matter of learning, but that learning is not complete until you've used it in action—by definition of learning. So part of that is taking part and learning to make a difference in the world in terms of networking with other people, formulating some plan, acting in however small a way to make a difference in the global sense. We have developed a series of strategies within that framework that do focus on the global issue, but that's a much more detailed response than your question calls for. We may want to come back to that in a good deal more detail in the next day or so.

VIRGINIA GRIFFIN: I was going to say one outcome of holistic or non-rational learning activity is often an awareness of one's connectedness to all of human kind. Which is a step towards peace in the world.

MAURICE GIBBONS: I think that the fulcrum point of the distinction between independence and interdependence *is* in values. I raised a point about spirituality this morning. And it's hard to raise that topic without seeming to also be raising some kind of specific point of view. I mean, small 's'—spirituality and values that are with that. I guess if we look upon learning-how-to-learn as a pursuit of independence, I still feel that the higher state is interdependence— that is, one must develop or have a sense of self in order to be able to stand outside the self and to see oneself as related to others. Actually I would see the two as highly interactive; one must develop as oneself in order to have a largeness, if you like, that enables one to see a greater importance than oneself. It takes a kind of self-confidence, a kind of self-awareness in order to be able to stand outside and see one's relationship with others.

The reason I see values as the fulcrum point between independence and interdependence is that as we develop, there is a larger set of questions, whether it's in the classroom working with physics or whether it's an independent project now or whether it's on the job trying to become more skillful or adapt to rapid change. It seems to me there's a larger framework within which these things happen that involves not only the increased skill or knowledge on the part of the person but the increased development of the self.

And by the development of the self, I mean something fairly specific; I mean that sense of those values we were talking about, those inner states that seem to be absolutely essential if a person is going to continue to develop independently. Those things like clarity about oneself, about one's meaning system. How can you set goals if you don't have that sense? And how do you develop a sense of that self if you're not determining what goals you are working toward? And a sense of confidence, a sense of openness - those kinds of qualities that are essential to be independent.

But those move within a framework that says: What am I moving toward? There is that larger question: What does my life mean? What am I moving toward? How am I evolving and toward what? So that the individual step really takes one to a larger framework of questions that reaches the most central that a human being can address. And it's by considering that larger sense even while we're considering the indivdual episode in physics class, at work or independently, in my own interest, whatever it may be, it is always within the context of moving toward: Who am I, Where am I going, and What am I going to become? And ultimately I see that associated with my sense of myself as a member of this world society, associating with a world population, addressing world issues and creating a kind of global future. And I think we are most powerful in cultivating learning-how-to-learn when we have that sense of a larger framework.

FREEDOM AND DEPENDENCE

RAVINDRA DAVE: Another thing that came up [in our subgroup] was that, as a result of competence building, consciousness raising, and confidence building, one begins to develop greater freedom. There is liberation in the whole process of learning and development. This is perhaps more of an outcome—that you are now less and less dependent. The school learning, the formal learning, has one great danger; the danger is that as you go through more and more of formal education you become more and more dependent on institutionalized learning. You become dependent on the teacher and the textbook, and unless you have an alternate framework you are not in a position to learn outside of school.

Now this is the negative impact of institutionalized and formalized learning. And what is needed is that while you are yet going through this instituionalized process of learning, you are working towards a set of competencies where without institutionalization, without having fixed plans (and so on), you can produce. And that involves a kind of freedom, flexibility, liberation, emancipation from ordinary school learning. So this was another point that came out.

Finally, according to my notes, all these things then—raising awareness, developing confidence, etc.—should then enable one to move gradually towards the peaks of excellence. The excellence is for the individual—that each person is in a position to reach the highest possible level. Now this level is to be determined on the basis of one's own previous limits. It is a sort of criterion reference approach rather than the type which asks how can you move from this stage to the highest possible externally sanctioned level of excellence.

MALCOLM KNOWLES: I have a deep conviction that we as educators have a primary obligation to help all people everywhere become self-directed learners. I find myself being reenforced with that conviction by a wonderful book that I wanted to bring to your attention. It's called *No Limits to Learning* [J.W. Botkin et al., Pergamon, 1979]. The main proposition is that in a world of accelerating change, as we have entered, it is not functional for educational systems to be turning out people who only have the competencies to deal with the world as it is now. They become obsolete rapidly. They call our present system maintenance education—providing people with the equipment to maintain things as they are now.

And they propose that in a world that is already changing we must reorganize our whole education system on the basis of "innovative education" or "anticipatory learning." And that the primary mission of formal education should be to develop the skills of learning. And then society should provide the resources for people to go on learning life-long. That makes good sense to me, given the kind of world we're entering.

RONALD CERVERO: Those are simply statements; that doesn't argue that there's not a value, that believing in learning-how-to-learn is not a value statement; it's merely giving the rationale as to why learning-how-to-learn should be supported.

MALCOLM KNOWLES: It's the basis of my valuing.

DAI HOUNSELL: I accept Ravi's notion about learning-how-to-learn—that it's an important function, preparing people for the unknown or coping with the problems of the rate at which knowledge becomes available and then obsolescent. I see another equally important function for it, and that's actually enabling people to learn better in the formal situations in which they already learn. And I think if we actually had tougher criteria for the outcomes of the experiences that people go through, much tougher criteria than we have now, we'd perceive much more widespread evidence of the failure of ourselves as teachers to really facilitate or enable learning by students under our control. Most of our formal procedures for testing, for examining, the grading and so on, don't really test understanding, analytical skills, all of the sorts of things that we talked about. So it seems to me that, if you like, a complementary (rather banal) function of learning-how-to-learn is actually to improve the quality of learning, perhaps by the quality of teaching.

ALAN KNOX: Any more comments on the value judgments that may in some instances throw in question our unbridled enthusiasm about the universal applicability of learning-how-to-learn?

MALCOLM KNOWLES: Never!

RONALD CERVERO: Well, I don't know whether these are values or assumptions that I've picked up as I look at these [items on the chalkboard]. One is that whatever this skill or personality construct is, it's something that can be picked up independent of the content—a generic skill that's independent of whatever it is that is to be learned. The second one is that it's applicable across a variety of situations. And the third is that it's enduring over time; that is, once you've learned it, you have it forever, or for a long period of time. Now I don't know whether those are values or assumptions underlying the concept.

VIRGINIA GRIFFIN: Do you question any of your statements?

RONALD CERVERO: I guess what I'm saying is that I don't know if there's empirical evidence to support those, but those are certainly the assumptions regarding the concept. And there may be empirical evidence that I'm not aware of.

ALAN KNOX: One easy example of learning-how-to-learn that we talked about a little bit this past evening is learning to read. And learning to read seems to me to fit your three assumptions very easily. Some of the other things we've talked about in those examples, perhaps less so.

ROBERT SMITH: I certainly don't agree with the last assumption. Many of the relevant skills require periodic review, refreshment and adaptations in contexts.

ALAN KNOX: And Ravi mentioned back-sliding in literacy campaigns in developing countries, a similar point.

RAVINDRA DAVE: One concern about values was raised yesterday: whether or not the skills and competencies of learning-how-to-learn will accentuate the tendency of education to produce inequality. Here there is a value orientation. Education produces inequalities even though in theory we say it should produce equality of opportunity, access and so on. In reality this happens. Now whether learning-how-to-learn will accentuate this process further is one aspect. The second part of it is connected.

We should examine the skills and the values associated with learning-how-to-learn and see whether or not, knowingly or inadvertently, we are overemphasizing, or reemphasizing, an elitist concept of society. For example, I would argue that while it is important, self learning (or self-directed) has this tendency of producing elitists—cutting them off, so to say, from the rest of the society. There's a need for emphasizing the aptitudes, the values and skills related to learning how to share one's learning with others.

Some people would like to keep learning to themselves. It becomes a part of property as it were. One has to learn how to share learning; in other words I would argue in favor of developing skills in what might be called inter-learning, or mutual learning. This is a very critical value-oriented, value-loaded issue. What kind of skills do you wish to foster?

ALAN KNOX: Earlier today our subgroup considered the notion that learning-how-to-learn and helping people to be more autonomous in learning represents progress. I think Roger [Säljö] raised the question that depending upon the societal setting, that may or may not represent progress. There's a value judgment there in terms of progress for the individual or progress for the society. And all of us tend to be so supportive of that idea that we tend not to examine the value judgments that are made accordingly.

EMANCIPATION AND PERSPECTIVE TRANSFORMATION

JEAN MOON: I have a question, and I wondered if you've included this in your thinking. This emancipation that was referred to, does it happen only after the person has looked at the assumptions they have held because of the culture and said, "I don't want those to be a part of my life anymore; I will move away from those assumptions?" Jack Mezirow (Mezirow, 1978) talks about emancipatory learning through a change in perspective. It involves looking at the assumptions on which you've based your life previously and saying that you don't like them and changing them. And I'm wondering if that's part of what you talked about—moving away from dependence on, for example, others' expectations.

ALAN KNOX: That question implied coming to an examination of who you are and how you fit in the larger society and coming up with some very different conclusions: that you're a victim, that the larger society is victimizing you and preventing some of that freedom and growth—that you've accepted in the past the rules of that larger society, your place in it, the stereotypes that are part of it and so on. And then seeing that process as a way of liberating oneself from the tyranny of those rules and assumptions. It seems to me that both can happen. You emphasized reinforcing the belief system and the assumptions and being stronger for it and Mezirow's emphasizing the transformation that can occur when you shift your perspective from accepting the given society, realize that rules are created by society and human beings and can be changed if you're willing to pay the price.

MAURICE GIBBONS: I think that what we are talking about, what seems to be a useful concept related to that, is the idea of dissonance. That really there is always some dissonance in a person's system. Now that can be, say, a sense of I am not being successful in this realm of my life. Or it can be I've got this vision that I want to pursue; it could be at opposite ends of the scale. So it's not necessarily one or the other. I think one of the things that we've found is that to emphasize the idea of becoming a better person is not a very healthy way to go at self-directed learning. Like saying what do you do least well and let's practice it. That seems to be the standard approach of the school—let's repeat what you do badly. It's better to say this is what you do well and let's do it and other things will be sucked into the wake. I think it's learning to pursue what you really do well and want to do well.

ALAN KNOX: Perspective transformation's concern is not so much trying to see the errors or the weaknesses or the shortcomings in yourself, but to realize how much you are being limited by accepting certain limitations in that larger society.

ETHICAL QUESTIONS

ROBERT SMITH: I see a values question coming in when we try, for example, to provide training interventions for the returning [to higher education] students. Do you train them to negotiate the system, get through as fast and as easily as possible? Or, do you train them for what our European friends call deeper, more meaningful learning and for looking at the curriculum as after all just a potential resource, all that kind of stuff? Seems to me it's almost an ethical issue. Do I give you the skills to slip through university and learn as little as possible and get out fast? Or do I take the high road?

RONALD CERVERO: Can't it be both?

DAI HOUNSELL: We British compromise in our comparable situation. We've found it a very difficult ethical problem. You have a problem when you come to understand how some students have adapted more successfully to the situation in which they find them-

selves. I'm putting that in a very euphemistic way.
A much blunter way would be that some students,
as you say, have wised up more successfully than
others. And that produces some problems about
the extent to which you encourage people to become aware of that.

On the other side, what one's trying to work at is
some kind of an educational or academic idea and
to gear learning-how-to-learn strategies towards
that. But clearly in some sense we have to do both.
Students are in situations where they have both kinds
of experiences—on the one hand very engaging,
very stimulating experiences which are perhaps just
not academic but involved their whole personality
in some way or another.

So in that sense, I suppose, one has to work with
both. But where that creates a problem, I think, is
that if I were to make some kind of value judgment
it's that wherever motivation is intrinsic rather than
extrinsic, it has more meaning for the people who
are concerned and they value more what they go
through. It seems to me you can't in a sense prepare
people for a situation in which they're so distanced
from what's going on and have so little personal
stake in it that the only kind of motivation they can
have is extrinsic (they're just there to get the grades,
to get the degree, to get the qualification some way
or other). That's a very soul destroying, mind numb-
ing, mind shrinking way of working. So I think we
have to sort of operate with both.

MAURICE GIBBONS: I've always assumed that learning-
how-to-learn was associated with and inseparable
from lifelong learning. That is, the reason why we
teach academically or in public education or on the
job is that essentially the learner will no longer be
dependent on the learning institution, whatever form
that may take and will be able to continue learning
on his or her own the rest of his or her life. That's
the empowering force behind learning-how-to-learn.

Is that a common agreement? It suddenly occurred to me that that might not be a common agreement.

ROBERT SMITH: Well, if I were running a medical school and I knew that the real dollars were in continuing medical education, I might want to turn the people out so dependent as learners that they'd come back regularly and pay five hundred dollars for two-day seminars. So I'd get the money needed to turn it into a research organization or to meet the equipment budget.

VIRGINA GRIFFIN: We were saying last night that learning-how-to-learn doesn't mean you are from then on independent and don't need help from anybody; that learning-how-to-learn may mean sometimes that I need the help of an educator, I need the help of a resource person right now to help me with this. So it doesn't mean we're working ourselves out of jobs completely. It may be that you could provide those five hundred dollar workshops and they would be most welcome by physicians who'd not been kept dependent as learners.

SOME EMERGING CONCLUSIONS AND AN ISSUE

Learning-How-to-Learn....

Is an overarching concept and an extensive knowledge domain

Is a lifelong process

Has relevance worldwide, in any nation or society

Should not be equated with study skills enhancement, nor with self-directed learning, nor with metacognition because the concept subsumes them

Has learner activeness and awareness at its core

Involves the acquisition and fostering of both generic and context-specific competencies

Implies as a central goal for all educational endeavor enhancement of capacity for further learning

Represents a means of empowerment

THE UMBRELLA TERM

The best overall descriptive term to employ when referring to the matters explored at the conference is an issue. Rubrics found in the literature include *metalearning* (not to be confused with metacognition, an aspect of the matter) and *learning-to-learn*, as well as *learning-how-to-learn.*

The matter was never really discussed, but Philip Candy took the trouble to build a case for learning-to-learn:

1. If learning is thought of simply as the receiving end of teaching, then "learning how to learn" is synonymous with "learning how to be taught." Although this is part of the concept, it is far from all of it.

2. If learning is thought of as "an increase in knowledge" or "memorizing," then the phrase "learning how to learn" must mean "learning how to increase knowledge," or "learning how to memorize," yet clearly it means much more than this. What is more, the word "learning" must have at least two quite different meanings, or else the phrase translates into "memorizing how to memorize" or "increasing knowledge about how to increase knowledge!"

3. If learning means roughly "an interpretive process aimed at the understanding of reality" (Roger Säljö), then "learning how to learn" means something like "an interpretive process aimed at understanding how to interpret and understand reality." While this is much richer, and more subtle, even it does not go far enough, because it ignores "learning *what* to learn," "learning *where* to learn," "learning *when* to learn" and, most important of all, "learning *why* to learn" or "*whether* to learn." The phrase "learning to learn" does not have this difficulty.

4. Finally, the phrase "learning to learn" can be read, and thought of, as "learning, to learn" or, in other words, "learning (in order) to learn." This implies the continuous nature of the process, which is something we have stressed in our discussions.

5. Thus, even though it is a small and probably pedantic point, I prefer "Learning to Learn" over "Learning How to Learn."

APPENDIX

The following are excerpts mailed in advance to the principals in order to stimulate dialogue and a reading list provided for persons attending the conference.

Statements About What Learning
How To Learn Involves
Sent to Principals as Pre-Conference Reading

Patricia Cross, "The Rising Tide of School Reform Reports," *Phi Delta Kappan* 66 (November 1984), 172

> How do we educate people to live in a world in which entire industries are created and wiped out in the short span of a single decade? The most important lessons that we can teach our children are the skills and the attitudes that will be required of lifelong learners. No education, no matter how brilliantly designed and delivered, will last a lifetime. The greatest handicap that any adult can have in the 21st century is a dislike of formal learning.

> It is already clear that a growing gap exists between adults who have learned to enjoy learning and to use it to make their lives richer (in every sense of that word) and adults who dislike learning and are stuck in dead-end (and even disappearing) jobs.

> If schools are to meet the foreseeable demands of the learning society, they will have to: 1) convince students that they are capable of learning and that learning is a useful and satisfying skill that will serve them well throughout their lives, 2) provide the cognitive skills that serve as the basic tools for lifelong learning, and 3) gradually put students in charge of their own learning, so that they can make wise choices from among the many learning options that will confront them as adults in the learning society.

Roger Säljö, "Learning about Learning," *Higher Education* 8 (1979), 446-51

In the accounts given by participants of their conception of learning and their methods of study there are, of course, all sorts of differences and similarities. My particular concern here is a very striking and, from a pedagogical point of view, very interesting difference between groups of people with respect to the perspective they have on learning. From our interviews it was clear that for some of the participants the phenomenon of learning in itself has become an object of reflection, while for others this is not the case. For some, learning is something which can be explicitly talked about and discussed and can be the object of conscious planning and analysis. In learning, these people realize that there are, for instance, alternative strategies or approaches which may be useful or suitable in various situations depending on, for example, time available, interest, demands of teachers and anticipated tests. To use a somewhat different terminology to describe this difference, for some people learning has become thematized, while for others the nature of learning is taken for granted. . . .

My guess. . . is that when people become aware of their own learning in different respects, they will be better equipped to deal with various sorts of learning difficulties. They may not become better learners within the context of a psychological laboratory with its constrained meaning of the context of learning, but I do think that they will become better at handling learning and reading problems of the kinds encountered in everyday life, or at least, in everyday studying.

Robert Smith, *Learning How to Learn* (Chicago: Follett, 1982), 17, 19, 25-26

For our purposes here, this definition should do: Learning how to learn involves possessing, or acquiring, the knowledge and skill to learn effectively in whatever learning situation one encounters. If you possess the necessary knowledge and skill, you've learned how to learn; and when you help yourself or others to acquire that kind of knowledge or skill, the concept is also at work.

The three subconcepts, or components, of the learning how to learn idea are the following: learners' needs (what learners need to know and be able to do for success in learning), learning style (a person's highly individualized preferences and tendencies that influence his or her learning), and training (organized activity, or instruction, to increase people's competence in learning). These supporting ideas of the concept of learning how to learn are interrelated. . . [and] they have important consequences— for both educational theory and practice, and implications for program development, teaching and learning.

Interrelated Subconcepts

Needs, learning style, and training—the three subconcepts of the learning how to learn concept—all are interrelated. We are only beginning to see how, but the outlines are clear. The first, needs, provides a way to focus on specific aspects of learning itself, what might be termed operational aspects as opposed to the more or less automatic processes involved. The focus is on key manageable (and "improvable") processes like planning, evaluating, and communicating. The second, learning style, goes far toward accounting for those individual differences in people that have the greatest implication for success in learning. Finally, organized efforts to foster success in learning constitute training. One requires knowledge about the needs and required competencies of the learner in order to train for improved learning performance; knowledge of the individual's learning style is helpful in doing so. A central training task becomes helping learners to gain insight into their styles and make useful adjustments in style.

Bruce Joyce, "Learning how to Learn," *Theory Into Practice* (1981), 26

Throughout one's life a human being encounters many teaching situations which require different responses. To the extent that we have not been taught the skills that enable us to adapt to a new approach we are deprived of learning in a serious way. People who have trouble relating to non-directive approaches are deprived of many of the benefits of counseling. People who cannot relate to models requiring social skills lose out in important areas of learning. Unless we have the skills of inductive thinking, inquiry oriented models leave us behind. Without the ability to relinquish control we fail to profit from behavioral systems approaches. One of the major tasks of schooling is to bring to students the skills that will widen for each of them the spectrum of learning environments to which they can relate. If we back off from an approach to teaching because the learner is initially incompatible with it we deprive the student of a life-long opportunity to learn from that approach. In an ideal world schooling would be organized to introduce learners systematically to a wider and wider repertoire of approaches to learning. The basic skills of learning how to learn should take their place with the basic skills of reading and arithmetic as the keys to a productive lifetime of personal growth.

Dai Hounsell, "Learning to Learn: Research and Development in Student Learning," *Higher Education* 8 (1979), 466

The relationship between research on student learning and the development of approaches to learning-to-learn is a complex one. While there are theoretical

links and points of correspondence between research findings and aspects of learning-to-learn approaches, the two areas have evolved in parallel
rather than hand-in-glove. Inevitably, the extent to
which research can inform learning-to-learn is cir-
cumscribed. The categorisation of qualitative differences in student learning is a case in point. Descriptions by researchers of qualitatively high approaches to learning—e.g., of "deep-level processing" or of "versatility"—can provide well-defined
criteria of outcomes and indicate characteristic
styles or strategies to which they are linked. Qualitatively low descriptive categories, on the other hand,
can help in the identification of weaknesses in the
way students tackle learning tasks but generally provide little indication of how these can be overcome.
The gap between diagnosis and remedy is often
large and may in some cases prove unbridgeable.
The phenomenon of learning is not accessible to
direct examination; it can only be studied obliquely,
through inferred or reported behaviour, or through
observation in experimental situations which, however realistic, are an incomplete mirror of reality.
More systematic observation of learning-to-learn activities, for example of conceptions of aspects of
learning which are apparent during course or workshop sessions, could provide an additional and
perhaps equally rich source of evidence about how
students perceive and approach their work.

Malcolm Knowles, *Modern Practice of Adult Education* (Chicago: Follett, 1980), 56

The important implication for adult-education practice of the fact that learning is an internal process
is that those methods and techniques which involve
the individual most deeply in self-directed inquiry
will produce the greatest learning. This principle of
ego-involvement lies at the heart of the adult
educator's art. In fact, the main thrust of modern
adult-educational technology is in the direction of

inventing techniques for involving adults in ever-deeper processes of self-diagnosis of their own needs for continued learning, in formulating their own objectives for learning, in sharing responsibility for designing and carrying out their learning activities, and in evaluating their progress toward their objectives.

Malcolm Knowles, "New Roles for Teachers—Empowerers of Lifelong Learners," *Journal of Children in Contemporary Society* 16 (1984), 85

In a world of accelerating change, education must be defined as a lifelong process of continuing inquiry. Accordingly, the most important of all—for both children and adults—is learning how to learn— acquiring the skills of self-directed inquiry.

Alan Knox, *Adult Development and Learning* (San Francisco: Jossey-Bass, 1977), 464, 468-69

Adults tend to underestimate their learning ability by overemphasizing their early school experience and underemphasizing their recent informal learning experiences. . . . Most of all, practitioners can help all adults realize that although there are substantial individual differences in learning ability, little of the variability is related to age. . . . Practitioners can help adults take optimistic, proactive and effective approaches to learning tasks and use reflection and learning episodes as ways to modify and direct their performance in action settings.

Ann Brown et al., "Learning to Learn: On Training Students to Learn from Texts," *Educational Researcher* (February, 1981), 16-17

Effective learning involves four main considerations: (1) the activities engaged in by the learner, (2) certain characteristics of the learner including his/her capacity and state of prior knowledge, (3) the nature of the materials to be learned, and (4) the critical task. In order for the psychologist or educator to devise a training program, it is necessary to consider all four aspects of the learning situation. . . . As psychologists, interested in understanding and promoting learning, we must appreciate the complex interaction implicit in this characterization of the learning situation, and we argue that this is exactly what the student must do. In order to become expert learners, students must develop some of the same insights as the psychologist into the demands of the learning situation. They must learn about their own cognitive characteristics, their available learning strategies, the demands of the various learning tasks and the inherent structure of the material. They must tailor their acvtivities finely to the competing demands of all these forces in order to become flexible and effective as learners. In other words, they must learn how to learn (Bransford, Stein, Shelton & Owings, 1980; Brown, 1980). As instructors our task should be to devise training routines that will help the student to develop the understanding of the learning situations. In principle, training can be aimed at all four points.

Carl Rogers, *A Way of Being* (Boston: Houghton Mifflin, 1980), 264, 266

There should be a place for learning by the whole person, with feelings and ideas merged. I have given much thought to this question of bringing together cognitive learning, which has always been needed, and affective-experiential learning, which is so underplayed in education today. . . . So if I were to attempt a crude definition of what it means to learn as a whole person, I would say that it involves learning of a unified sort, at the cognitive, feeling, and gut levels, with a clear awareness of the different aspects of this unified learning.

Philip Candy, *A Personal Construct Approach to Adult Learning*, (Adelaide College of the Arts and Education, Underdale, South Australia, 1980), 44

Learning about one's own learning processes is

among the higher forms of 'personal knowledge', and therefore the techniques for presenting, elucidating and discussing 'public knowledge' are entirely inappropriate. Whilst generalisations about 'learning styles' or cognitive processes may prove useful as ways of viewing learning, their value really is limited to assisting the individual to perceive his own learning in a new way. . . . Clearly. . .it is not the purpose of learning to learn programmes, to create a situation of dependency, where the learner constantly needs a mentor to guide and monitor his learning processes. To the contrary, the ultimate intention is to produce self-organized and self-aware learners.

Graham Gibbs, *Teaching Students To Learn* (Milton Keynes, England: The Open University Press, 1981), 87-88

I believe that telling students how to learn is not often justifiable or effective, and I believe that developments in students' fundamental conceptions of learning underlie developments in their practical studying behavior. But linking these two beliefs and providing a rationale for my strategies is a broader set of beliefs concerning how people develop and change, how they learn at all, rather than beliefs specifically concerned with studying. These beliefs are based largely in constructivist notions (e.g., the personal construct theory of George Kelly, 1959) and in humanistic psychology (e.g., Carl Rogers's notions concerning learning, Rogers, 1969). Without labouring the point, I believe people construct their own worlds. New constructions, new understandings and ways of seeing things, are based on existing constructions and ways of seeing things. I do not see how a person's understanding can significantly develop without involving their existing conceptions, however crude and 'wrong' these are. Also I see significant learning as involving a degree of disorientation and personal threat, and requiring personal autonomy and responsibility from the learner. Developing as a learner is a continuous process, and unless the student takes responsibility for this process—for becoming aware of how he is learning and noticing what works and what does not—then change will be impeded. Instead of making students dependent on expert advice and evaluation, self-evaluation and self-awareness should be encouraged. Only when students can see for themselves what the advantages and disadvantages of different ways of going about a study task are is development likely.

Allen Tough, *The Adult's Learning Projects* (Austin, TX: Learning Concepts, 1971), 148-49

Many schools and colleges claim that they teach their students how to learn, and prepare them for a lifetime of adult learning. They should state these objectives more precisely, do everything possible to encourage and help their students attain them, and measure the extent to which their graduates exhibit these behaviors several years after leaving.

These objectives can be stated in behavioral terms as follows:

1. As a result of his experiences in this educational institution, the student will tend to initiate a learning project when facing a major problem or task, and when experiencing strong puzzlement or curiosity. He will use learning as one step in achieving certain goals in his home and family, in his leisure activities, and on the job.
2. The student will realize that learning projects are common, natural, and useful. He will be aware that people learn for a variety of reasons, that most learning is not for credit, and that each type of planner is appropriate in certain circumstances. He will not regard any reason for learning, or any type of planner, as strange or inferior. He will not believe that learning with a professional teacher in an educa-

tional institution is the only way to learn, and will not feel guilty when he chooses other formats for learning.

3. The student will become much more competent at discovering and setting his personal life goals and learning goals, at choosing the planner for his learning project, at conducting his own self-planned projects, at defining the desired help and getting it from a person or group, at learning from nonhuman resources, and at evaluating his progress and efficiency in a learning project.

Conference Reading List

Apps, J. W. *Study Skills for Those Adults Returning to School*. New York: McGraw-Hill, 1978.

Benne, Kenneth, et al. *The Laboratory Method of Changing and Learning*. Palo Alto, CA: Science and Behavior Books, 1975.

Bergevin, P. E. and McKinley, J. *Participation Training for Adult Education*. St. Louis: The Bethany Press, 1967.

Birkey, J. Moon. "Future Directions for Adult Education and Adult Educators. *Journal of Teacher Education* 35 (1984): 25-29.

Boud, D. *Developing Student Autonomy in Learning*. New York: Nichols, 1981.

Brookfield, S. "Learning to Learn: The Characteristics, Motivations, and Destinations of Adult Study Skills Students." *Adult Education* 50 (1978): 363-68.

Brookfield, S. "Independent Adult Learning," *Studies in Adult Education* 13 (1981): 15-27.

Brookfield, S. "Self-directed Learning: A Critical Review of Research," in S. Brookfield, ed. *Self-Directed Learning: Theory and Practice* San Francisco: Jossey-Bass, 1985, 5-15.

Brown, A. L., et al. "Learning to Learn: On Training Students to Learn from Texts." *Educational Researcher* (February 1981): 14-21.

Brown A. L. and Palincsar, A. S. "Reciprocal Teaching of Comprehension Strategies: A Natural History of One Program for Enhancing Learning" in J. Borkowski and J. D. Day, eds., *Intelligence and Cognition in Special Children: Comparative Studies of Giftedness, Mental Retardation, and Learning Disabilities*. New York: Ablex, in press.

Brundage, D. H. and MacKeracher, D. *Adult Learning Principles and Their Application to Program Planning*. Toronto: Ontario Ministry of Education, 1980.

Bruner, J. S. *The Process of Education*. New York: Vintage, 1963.

Buzan, T. *Use Your Head*. London: British Broadcasting Association, 1973.

Candy, P. C. *A Personal Construct Approach to Adult Learning*. Underdale, South Australia: Adelaide College of the Arts and Education, 1980.

Candy P. C. "Personal Constructs and Personal Learning Style" in T. R. Keen and M. L. Pope, eds., *Practical Educational Applications of the Repertory Grid*. Montreal: Cybersystems, 1985.

Cell, E. *Learning to Learn From Experience*. Albany: State University of New York Press, 1984.

Cross, K. P. *Adults as Learners*. San Francisco: Jossey-Bass, 1981.

Cross, K. P. "The Rising Tide of School Reform Reports." *Phi Delta Kappan* 66 (1984): 167-72.

Dave, R. H. *Lifelong Education and School Curriculum*. UIE Monographs No. 1. Hamburg: UNESCO Institute for Education, 1973.

Dodd, A. W. "A New Design for Public Education." *Phi Delta Kappan 65 (1984): 685-87.*

Dunn, R. and Price, G. Teaching Students Through Their Individual Learning Styles. Reston, VA: Reston Publishing Company, 1978.

Entwistle N. J. "Identifying Distinctive Approaches to Studying." *Higher Education* 8 (1979): 365-80.

Entwistle, N. J. and Hounsell, D. "Student Learning in Its Natural Setting." *Higher Education* 8 (1979): 359-63.

Entwistle, J. J. and Wilson, J. D. *Degrees of Excellence*. London: Hodder and Stoughton, 1977.

Ferguson, M. *The Acquarian Conspiracy: Personal and Social Transformation in the 1980s*. Los Angeles: J. P. Tarcher, 1980.

Ford, N. "Recent Approaches to the Study and Teaching of 'Effective Learning' in Higher Education." *Review of Educational Research* 51 (1981): 345-77.

Freire, P. *The Pedagogy of the Oppressed*. New York: Seabury Press, 1974.

Freire, P. *Education for Critical Consciousness*. New York: Continuum Books (Seabury Press), 1974.

Gibbons, M., Bailey, A., Comeau, P., Schmuck, J., Seymour, S., and Wallace, D. "Toward A Theory of Self-Directed Learning: A Study of Experts Without Formal Training." *Journal of Humanistic Psychology* 20, 2 (1980): 41-56.

Gibbons, M. and Phillips, G. "Self-Education: The Process of Life-Long Learning." *Canadian Journal of Education* 7, 4 (1982): 67-86.

Gibbs, G. *Teaching Students to Learn*. Milton Keynes, England: The Open University Press, 1981.

Gibbs, G., Morgan, A. and Taylor, E. *Why Students Don't Learn*. Report from Study Methods Group, Institute of Educational Technology. Milton Keynes, England: The Open University Press, 1982.

Griffin, V. *Through a Glass Brightly. A New Image of Learners and Learning*. Technical report. Toronto: Department of Education, Ontario Institute for Studies in Education, 1981.

Gross, R. *The Lifelong Learner.* New York: Simon and Schuster, 1977.

Hamblin, D. H. *Teaching Study Skills.* Oxford: Basil Blackwell, 1981.

Harri-Augstein, S. E. and Thomas, L. F. *Reading to Learn.* London: Methuen, 1982.

Houle, C. O. *Continuing Your Education.* New York: McGraw-Hill, 1964.

Houle, C. O. *Patterns of Learning.* San Francisco: Jossey-Bass, 1984.

Hounsell, D. "Learning to Learn: Research and Development in Student Learning." *Higher Education* 8 (1979): 453-69.

Joyce, B. "Learning How to Learn." *Theory into Practice* 19 (1981): 15-27.

Joyce, B. and Weil, M. *Models of Teaching,* Englewood Cliffs, NJ: Prentice-Hall, 1980.

Keeton, M. T., ed. *Experiential Learning: Rationale, Characteristics, and Assesment.* San Francisco: Jossey-Bass, 1976.

Kelly, G. A. *The Psychology of Personal Constructs.* 2 Vols. New York: Norton, 1955.

Kirby, P. *Cognitive Style, Learning Style, and Transfer Skill Acquisition.* Columbus, OH: National Center for Research in Vocational Education, 1979.

Kirchenbaum, D. S. and Perri, M. G. "Improving Academic Competence in Adults: A Review of Recent Research." *Journal of Counseling Psychology* 29 (1982): 76-94.

Knowles, M. S. *Self-Directed Learning.* New York: Association Press, 1975.

Knowles, M. S. *The Modern Practice of Adult Education.* Chicago: Association Press, Follett Publishing Company, 1980.

Knowles, M. S. "New Roles for Teachers-Empowerers of Lifelong Learners." *Journal of Children in Contemporary Society* 16 (1984): 85-94.

Knox, A. B. *Adult Development and Learning.* San Francisco: Jossey-Bass, 1977.

Knox, A. B., ed. "Enhancing Proficiencies of Adult Educators." *New Directions for Continuing Education 1.* Jossey-Bass, 1979.

Kolb, D. A. *Experiential learning.* Englewood Cliffs, NJ: Prentice-Hall, 1984.

Lewis, D. and Greene, J. *Thinking Better.* New York: Rawson, Wade, 1982.

Marton, F. "Studying Conceptions of Reality—A Metatheoretical Note." *Scandinavian Journal of Educational Research 25 (1981): 159-69.*

Marton, F., Hounsell, D., and Entwistle, N. eds. *The Experience of Learning.* Edinburgh: Scottish Academic Press, 1984.

Marton, F. and Säljö, R. "On Qualitative Differences in Learning, I. Outcome and Process." *British Journal of Educational Psychology* 46 (1976): 4-11.

Mezirow, J. "Perspective Transformation." *Adult Education* 28 (1978): 100-109.

Mezirow, J. "A Critical Theory of Self-Directed Learning." In S. Brookfield, ed., *Self-Directed Learning: Theory and Practice.* San Francisco: Jossey-Bass, 1985, pp. 17-30.

National Association of Secondary School Principals. *Student Learning Styles.* Reston, VA: NASSP, 1979.

Novak, J. D. and Gowin, D. B. *Learning How to Learn.* New York: Cambridge University Press, 1984.

Ostrander, S. and Schroeder, L. *Superlearning.* New York: Dell, 1979.

Perry, W. G., Jr. *Forms of Intellectual and Ethical Development in the College Years.* New York: Holt, Rinehart and Winston, 1970.

Roberts, T. B. *Four Psychologies Applied to Education.* New York: John Wiley, 1975.

Roberts, T. B. "Expanding Thinking Through Consciousness Education." *Educational Leadership* 39 (1981): 52-54.

Rogers, C. *A Way of Being.* Boston: Houghton Mifflin, 1980.

Rogers, C. *Freedom to Learn.* Columbus, OH: Charles E. Merrill, 1969.

Smith, R. M. *Helping Adults Learn How to Learn.* San Francisco: Jossey-Bass, 1983.

Smith, R. M. and Haverkamp, K. "Toward a Theory of Learning How to Learn." *Adult Education* 28 (1977): 3-21.

Tough, A. *The Adult's Learning Projects*, 2nd Edition Austin, TX: Learning Concepts, 1979.

Tough, A. *Intentional Changes: A Fresh Approach to Helping People Change.* Chicago: Follett, 1982.

Walsh, R. and Vaughan, F. *Beyond Ego: Transpersonal Dimensions in Psychology.* Los Angeles: J. P. Tarcher, 1980.

Säljö, R. "Learning About Learning." *Higher Education* 8 (1979): 443-51.

Säljö, R. "Learning Approach and Outcome: Some Empirical Observations." *Instructional Science* 10 (1981): 47-65.

Sanders, P. and Yanouzas, J. N. "Socialization to Learning." *Training and Development Journal* (July, 1983): 14-21.

Skrager, R. *Organizing Schools To Encourage Self-Direction in Learners.* UNESCO Institute for Education. New York: Pergamon Press, 1984.

Smith, R. M. *Learning How to Learn in Adult Education.* (Report No. 10: 1976). DeKalb, IL: ERIC Clearinghouse in Career Education, (ERIC Document Reproduction Service No. ED 132 245) 1976.

Smith, R. M. *Learning How to Learn: Applied Theory for Adults.* Chicago: Follett, 1982.

Index